HEALTHY VEGAN, HAPPY BODY

HEALTHY VEGAN, HAPPY BODY

THE COMPLETE PLANT-BASED COOKBOOK
FOR A WELL-NOURISHED LIFE

TESS CHALLIS

ROCKRIDGE
PRESS

For general information on our other products and services or to obtain tech-nical support, please contact our Customer Care Department within the United States at (866) 744-2665, or outside the United States at (510) 253-0500.

Rockridge Press publishes its books in a variety of electronic and print for-mats. Some content that appears in print may not be available in electronic books, and vice versa.

Interior and Cover Designer: Angie Chiu
Art Producer: Hannah Dickerson
Editor: Reina Glenn
Production Editor: Andrew Yackira

Photography © 2020 Iain Bagwell, food styling by Loren Wood, cover and pp. II, VI, VIII, X, 8, 20, 38, 58, 78, 85, 93, 98, 114, 121, 127, 132, 149, 154, 161, 167, 172, 179, 189, 196, 209, 214; © Ray Kachatorian, p. 27; © Helene Dujardin, pp. 33, 73, 105; © Nadine Greeff, p. 45; © Kate Lewis, p. 143; iStock/bhofack2, p. 53; Shut-terstock/Anna Shepulova, p. 65; Stocksy/Laura Adani, p. 111; Stocksy/Susan Brooks-Dammann, p. 203. Author photo courtesy of Melissa Schwartz.

ISBN: Print 978-1-64611-880-9 | eBook 978-1-64611-881-6

R0

This book is dedicated to you. I truly hope it will inspire you to love the foods that love you back!

CONTENTS

INTRODUCTION

I've been every kind of vegan—clinically obese, binge-eating, orthorexic, and even that annoyingly judgy vegan (apologies to everyone I spoke to in 1991—there are none so righteous as the newly converted). That was the year I gave up animal products and discovered that my body thanked me for it, no longer vexing me with chronic illness, never-ending acne, anemia, and lethargy.

In the beginning, I was a pretty healthy vegan, but within a few years, that turned into an obsession with being perfect. I convinced myself that all oils, salts, fats, nuts, and even tofu were off-limits. That was my orthorexia phase, which eventually ping-ponged to binge eating, due to my basic human desire for delicious food. I'd tell myself I couldn't have even a minimal amount of olive oil, guacamole, or tofu, yet I'd end up bingeing on onion rings, vegan chocolate cake, and potato chips. I'd tell myself, "I'll be perfect tomorrow, so just for today, I'll eat the stuff I can't eat later on." I repeated that nonsense every day for years.

You'd think I would have figured out that I was lying to myself, but it wasn't until I was diagnosed as clinically obese at age 28 that I finally realized how unhealthy I'd gotten. At that point, I decided to try a diet that emphasized plant-strong whole foods, but also allowed for some treats now and then, without the guilt. I gave myself full permission to eat tofu (I was really getting wild, huh?), avocados, chocolate, and even oils in moderation. By finding a diet that included some wiggle room, I could actually stick with it, and I was able to drop the excess weight. What a joyful realization to know that I could not only be healthy, but also eat foods I loved every single day.

Since then, I've learned I wasn't alone in that type of behavior. I've coached hundreds of people who can relate to this, because they've been through it—so if this sounds familiar to you, please know you're not alone. It's all too common for people to live in a state of "binge and restrict," due to unrealistic dietary expectations. Deprivation doesn't work and absolutely does not need to be part of your lifestyle in order for you to be healthy. One of my greatest passions is sharing recipes that show just how scrumptious healthy, plant-based foods can be, and also how easy they can be to make. You don't have to sacrifice flavor *or* your health—isn't that awesome?

In this book, I'll be sharing some of my new favorite recipes with you, along with tips on how to set up your kitchen, prep healthy food, and make the most of your meals. It's my hope that you will fall in love with these recipes, and that they will be a huge contribution to your taste buds, well-being, and whole life. Cheers to healthy, happy living!

CHAPTER ONE

FALLING IN LOVE WITH VEGAN COOKING

Let's start with a question that's being asked a lot these days: What's so great about vegan eating? There are a plethora of answers, but the one we'll be focusing on here is that the food is beyond amazing. When I first went vegan almost three decades ago, I was worried I'd be missing out. But I soon found that the flavors available in the plant-based world were uniquely satisfying. So, buckle up, because you're entering plant paradise. You'll be so glad you moved to this happy, healthy land.

HOW PLANT-BASED FOODS SATISFY EVERY TASTE BUD

Before going vegan, I imagined vegans dining on nothing but salads, salads, and did I mention, salads? Thankfully, I was oh-so wrong. Somehow vegan food has gotten a reputation for being unsatisfying and bland, but that's because most people focus on what's *missing* from their plates, versus what's actually present.

I'd love to dispel a myth right here and now: You absolutely do not have to give up the flavors you love in order to eat a vegan diet. The world of flavor has five major categories, and you can find them all in the plant kingdom. Know how to balance them, and you'll be able to make dishes that satisfy your soul as well as your taste buds. Not to mention, it will help you become an intuitively great cook.

SALTY

Oh, salt. You get such a bad rap. While most of us do consume too much sodium (90 percent of Americans, in fact), it's usually from packaged, processed foods and restaurant meals. The good news? Cooking at home using whole-food ingredients allows you to add salt to your meals in moderation without the guilt. I am definitely a pro-salt person, because it brings out the wonderful flavors of any dish (even desserts).

SWEET

Sugar might have an even worse reputation than salt. But, as with salt, the type and quantity of sweetness you consume is what matters most. Again, if you're making your food at home and using healthy recipes such as the ones in this book—as well as listening to your body—you can enjoy both great health and delicious desserts. The sweet element in a dish can also be a great way to balance savory or spicy flavors (such as a touch of maple syrup in a Thai peanut sauce or a spicy chili).

BITTER

When you think of bitter flavors, you might not always imagine delectable food, but bitterness can actually be key to balancing certain dishes—the trick is pairing it with complementary flavors. For example, some of the best chocolate desserts incorporate bitter chocolate with a high percentage of cocoa. Another bitter flavor I really enjoy is turmeric, which is delicious when paired with lemon, ginger, and a little sweetness like in the Anti-Inflammatory Tonic (page 22).

SOUR

This is one of the most overlooked flavor components, but it's so important. Sourness can make a bland dish pop and balance out earthy flavors (there's a reason why there's lime or lemon in all of my fresh green juices, especially those containing beets or carrots). You can achieve that sourness with citrus and all sorts of vinegars.

UMAMI

Umami is the "savory" element that gives certain dishes their grounded, full-bodied flavor. Healthy vegan versions of umami include mushrooms (especially intensely flavored ones such as shiitake), caramelized onions, soy sauce, and ripe tomatoes. Although vegan, MSG is generally considered both umami and unhealthy, so I'd suggest sticking with the more natural sources of this great flavor component.

NUTRITION BASICS

People often get nervous about nutrition when they transition to a plant-based diet. They especially wonder if they'll get enough iron, calcium, protein, and B₁₂. When I first went vegan in 1991, I too was worried about getting enough nutrients.

What I discovered greatly eased my mind: If we're eating a plant-based diet composed mostly of whole foods (and are getting enough calories), it's very easy to meet all of our nutritional needs. *Isn't that great news?* I don't take any supplements, and every time I've had my nutrient levels tested over the decades, they've always been high. Organic vegetables, fruits, and whole plant foods are all I need to stay healthy. However, if you're not comfortable with my no-supplements approach, do what works best for you. All of the recipes in this book have nutritional information, so you'll see exactly what you're getting.

PROTEIN

Ah, the favorite question every vegan hears: "Where do you get your protein?" And the answer? "Everywhere—and in great quantities!" It's actually hard *not* to get enough protein, unless you're undereating in general. In fact, *all* plant-based foods contain protein— even strawberries contain 8 percent protein. Plant-based foods with the highest protein content include tofu, tempeh, edamame,

lentils, beans, nuts, quinoa, chia seeds, hemp seeds, potatoes, and vegetables like broccoli, kale, and mushrooms.

IRON AND ZINC

Iron is another mineral that vegans should easily get plenty of—it's prevalent in greens, legumes, seeds, and nuts. I personally went from being an anemic ovo-lacto vegetarian to having high levels of iron after switching to a vegan diet. Since meat is high in iron and dairy products contain zero iron, it's common to experience a drop in iron when you give up meat and substitute dairy. However, a plant-based diet based primarily on whole foods is naturally rich in iron. Zinc is also easy to obtain on a vegan diet—find it in pumpkin seeds, tofu, hemp, lentils, oats, wild rice, and more.

OMEGA-3 FATTY ACIDS

Omega-3s are essential for brain function and also have anti-inflammatory benefits. Omega-3s are, surprise, also abundant in plant-based foods. These essential fatty acids are prevalent in flaxseed, walnuts, algae, hemp seeds, chia seeds, and more. Again, simply by eating a varied, whole foods–based vegan diet (with enough calories, and including the healthy fats mentioned above), you should naturally be getting enough omega-3s.

CALCIUM

Interestingly, calcium is another nutrient that people have mistakenly relied on dairy products for. However, this vital mineral is abundant in many vegan foods. Foods rich in calcium include sesame seeds, tofu, soy, legumes and beans, and vegetables such as broccoli, Brussels sprouts, collards, kale, mustard greens, Swiss chard, and turnip greens.

VITAMIN D

Call me old fashioned, but I like to get my Vitamin D from its source—the sun! If you get adequate (yet not excessive) amounts of sunshine, Vitamin D shouldn't be a problem for you. However, for those who live in sunshine-challenged areas, there are always Vitamin D–fortified products on the market. Look for it in juices, plant milks, and cereals.

Vitamin B12

The only supplement I personally advocate on a plant-based diet is B12. It's stored in the body for long periods of time, so a daily supplement isn't necessary—a few times per month should do the trick. Or, you can simply eat fortified nutritional yeast with high amounts of B12 on a regular basis, which is what I do. The average recommended B12 intake for adults is 1–25 mcg per day.

THE HEALTHY VEGAN PHILOSOPHY

Just because someone is vegan doesn't mean they're healthy. I was clinically obese as a vegan during most of my 20s, eating primarily processed foods—white breads, refined sugars, fried foods, and almost no vegetables. Ironically, this state came about because I was trying to be "too healthy" and ended up bingeing on junk food due to feeling deprived all the time. I had decided I needed to eschew *all* oils at *all* times, and even healthy fats such as avocados were on my no-no list. It wasn't until I allowed myself to eat in a balanced way, while emphasizing whole foods and plenty of vegetables, that I regained a healthy weight.

After working with countless people over the years on the subjects of food, eating, and health, I encourage you to define what healthy means to you. We are all in different places, and we must honor exactly where we're at, with an eye on constant improvement. I'm a huge fan of the "progress, not perfection" mentality. A happy side effect is that the healthier we eat, the more our taste buds evolve and our bodies begin craving healthier foods. Healthy habits build on themselves.

So, what does a "healthy" vegan diet mean these days? To me, it's about eating as many nutrient-dense whole foods as possible—filling up on fresh fruits, vegetables, legumes, and whole grains, as well as enjoying nuts, seeds, and avocados. I also find that vegan treats are fine in moderation, when eaten mindfully.

However, there are some foods I recommend limiting in pursuit of a healthy lifestyle, and they likely won't come as a surprise.

WHITE FLOUR

White flour is something I personally avoid, due to its lack of nutrients and fiber. It's found in breads, tortillas, and baked goods (to name a few), and often labeled deceptively as "wheat flour." If you want whole-grain flour, you'll need to look for the word "whole" in the ingredients list. The good news is that there are lots of great alternatives to white flour. For baking, whole-wheat pastry flour is an excellent stand-in.

OIL

Oy. Oils. We've now entered a zone that contains a million different perspectives, and a lot of heated debates. My take? A low-fat, plant-strong diet with minimal oils is just fine. I do not personally feel it's necessary to make them completely off-limits—and as I mentioned previously, I've found it detrimental to do so. I enjoy many oil-free foods, yet also find that a splash of oil here and there can make a dish much more satisfying. For example, a teaspoon of toasted sesame oil can bring a stir-fry to life and give it depth of flavor.

Essentially, I recommend adding the minimum amount of oil necessary in order to make your food taste great. I personally keep a teaspoon handy while I'm cooking so that I'm not wantonly pouring oil into my pans. I find that a teaspoon or so is often plenty to round out the flavors. I also recommend using high-quality organic oils, such as olive, sunflower, sesame, and coconut, rather than soybean, canola, or "vegetable oil."

As with anything, take in this information, check in with your own wisdom, and find what works for you—making sure it's something you can realistically (yes, really, really realistically) stick with. We're all different, and no one needs to be perfect in order to be vibrantly healthy.

REFINED SUGAR

I swore off refined sugar about seven years ago, after discovering (via an incident with a cupcake . . . or three) how much it seemed to affect my immune system, energy, and the appearance of my skin. I went on to learn that sugar has been linked to cellular aging, depression, reduced energy, weight gain, and heart disease (to name a few). Luckily, I've never looked back, as those reasons all motivated me tremendously.

The great thing about avoiding refined sugar is that it's actually pretty easy to replace. I've found that natural sweeteners such as maple syrup, coconut sugar, brown rice syrup, and even our controversial friend, agave nectar, tend to give plenty of sweetness without the negative side effects of cane sugar.

Reducing or eliminating sugar can seem daunting at first, because it seems like it's in everything—baked goods, breads, sauces, cereals, and even ketchup. But don't despair. Once you get used to reading labels, you can find delicious alternatives, especially if you're cooking at home and using the recipes in this book.

PROCESSED PRODUCTS

At the risk of sounding like a broken record, I don't want to encourage some idea of perfection here. You don't need to avoid *all* processed foods at *all* times in order to

THE WHOLE-FOODS, PLANT-BASED DIET

There's a lot of confusion around the difference between veganism and a whole-foods, plant-based (WFPB) diet. Veganism is the exclusion of all animal products, which includes both food (eggs, dairy, meat, fish, poultry, and honey) and clothing (wool, silk, leather, and fur). A vegan diet can include a range of nutrient-dense foods; however, it can just as easily consist of processed foods such as packaged vegan meats, cheeses, chips, and ice cream.

On the other hand, a whole-foods, plant-based diet is made of strictly nutrient-dense foods such as fruits, vegetables, whole grains, legumes, nuts, and seeds, with *no processed foods of any sort*. Some people apply flexibility to the word *based* in "whole-foods, plant-based" and occasionally consume animal products. But for the purposes of this book, a WFPB diet is one that excludes all animal products and emphasizes whole, nutrient-dense foods over processed foods.

There are varying degrees of a WFPB diet as well, with the strictest sense excluding all oils, sugars, and salt. As you may have guessed, I take a more moderate approach, so you will see minimal amounts of oil and sea salt in several recipes. However, if you prefer the strict approach, there are WFPB tips at the bottom of many of the recipes in this book to help you modify.

be healthy. In fact, almost everything we eat is "processed." For example, a can of organic pinto beans is, in fact, processed. It's not in the state of the original bean. Those beans have been cooked, canned, and shipped. However, for the purposes of this book, processed products mean foods that have additives and fillers—the kind that are truly less than ideal. And even if you're vegan, there are a lot of these products on the market, disguised by their convenience (both a blessing and a curse).

Some common examples include veggie burgers, vegan meats and cheeses, frozen dinners, chips, packaged cookies, and *so much more*. Of course, some processed products are much healthier than others. There are frozen veggie burgers made from whole foods that I endorse, but plenty of others are mostly made from nonorganic soy or wheat by-products, with lots of preservatives and ingredients you can't pronounce.

In general, I suggest looking for products that contain whole-foods ingredients, ideally organic, without preservatives or artificial ingredients, and without excess oils or refined sugars. Look for whole grains, legumes, nuts, seeds, vegetables, and fruits as the stars of the show. Again, back to reading the good old ingredients list.

THE BENEFITS OF HEALTHY EATING

We all know we should eat healthfully, but sometimes we need a little extra motivation. Here are some of the reasons why choosing a healthy plant-based diet is the gift that keeps on giving.

SAVING MONEY

You may have heard that making the switch from the standard American diet (SAD) to veganism is *more* expensive, despite cutting out pricey meat purchases. That can be true, but vegetables (even organic ones) usually aren't what breaks the bank—it's the packaged vegan products that are expensive. When I'm at the grocery store and all of my whole-food items (beans, oats, vegetables, etc.) go through the line, the total is modest. It's when my specialty items (kombucha, gourmet vegan cheese, superfood powder, etc.) get tacked on that the total skyrockets. While spending lots of money on premade vegan products is easy, the essentials of a plant-based diet are actually very reasonably priced. If you're on a budget, you can save money by focusing on whole foods like beans and whole grains that you can purchase in bulk.

PREVENTING DISEASE

An awesome thing happens when you adopt a healthy plant-based diet—you become much more immune to illness and disease. According to a study funded by the National Institute of Health/National Cancer Institute, vegans have the lowest risk of cancer, heart disease, and hypertension. Dr. Caldwell Esselstyn Jr., who directs the cardiovascular prevention and reversal program at the Cleveland Clinic Wellness Institute, says you can become "heart attack proof" on a healthy plant-based diet, despite your genetics. Numerous studies also show that a vegan diet can prevent type 2 diabetes.

BOOSTING ENERGY

Unfortunately, so many people deal with low energy on a daily basis that it's become a social norm. I can vividly recall what it felt like back in my teens, struggling to stay awake in English class after lunch, my head so heavy it felt impossible not to lie down on my desk. Food was something that practically knocked me unconscious.

One of the things I noticed immediately upon going vegan was that my energy levels increased dramatically. No more afternoon dips, no more sluggish mornings. This is because plant-based protein takes less time for the body to process than animal protein, meaning you're back on your feet quicker after a vegan meal. So, even if you can't remember what it feels like to have boundless energy throughout the day, a healthy plant-based diet can be your saving grace.

REDUCING INFLAMMATION

According to a study funded by the National Institute of Health/National Cancer Institute, vegans have higher levels of omega-3 fatty acids, carotenoids, and isoflavones—all of which are associated with lower inflammation. However, the type of vegan you are greatly impacts this result. I've noticed that when I avoid sugars, refined flours, and most processed foods—as well as increase inflammation-fighting foods such as ginger and turmeric—my inflammation level is much lower. How can I tell? My joints aren't stiff or achy, my exercise recovery is much more rapid, and my skin isn't puffy (hey, vanity can be a valid reason to eat healthy!). Lower inflammation can even mean a significant reduction in arthritis pain.

CHAPTER TWO

STOCK AND PREP

If you're feeling panicky about transitioning to a plant-based diet, here's a helpful reminder: You likely have lots of the ingredients you'll need on hand already. Oats, black pepper, popcorn? Check, check, check! Get started with what you have in your cabinet and incorporate the new items as you go. This chapter will help you transform your kitchen to take on any and all plant-based recipes.

EQUIPMENT

You won't need to spend loads of money on new tools to cook the recipes in this book, but I'd be remiss if I didn't share my favorites with you. Certain gadgets can make your plant-based lifestyle much easier.

MUST-HAVES

There are certain items you simply must have in order to make the most of the upcoming recipes:

- Blender
- Chef's knife
- Citrus press
- Cutting boards
- Food processor
- Graters (for regular and fine vegetable grating)
- Measuring cups and spoons
- Mixing bowls
- Pots and pans
- Spatulas
- Wire whisk

NICE-TO-HAVES

These items aren't required, but oh-so nice to have. They'll help you save time and create even better results.

- Air fryer
- Electric juicer
- Food dehydrator
- Garlic press
- High-speed blender
- Instant Pot
- Mandoline
- Rice cooker
- Toaster oven

PANTRY

Having a well-stocked pantry is invaluable when transitioning your diet. When you've got the basics on hand, it's so much easier to whip up a soup, entrée, or dressing. Then, your weekly shopping list consists mainly of produce items and the occasional replacement when a pantry item is getting low. Here's what to keep in stock.

BEANS AND LENTILS

In my kitchen, you'll find both dry and canned lentils and beans. The lentils are easy to cook in a standard pot for soups, and the beans do well in an Instant Pot or on the stove. For canned beans, I use Eden brand, as they have the best practices (cooking the beans with kombu for better digestion and using high-quality ingredients, etc.). These are good varieties to keep on hand:

- Black beans
- Black-eyed peas
- Chickpeas
- Lentils (red and brown)
- Pinto beans
- White or navy beans
- Yellow split peas

GRAINS

Several grains will appear throughout the book, including the ones that follow. Brown rice is a staple of mine—if you only want to buy one kind, the short-grain variety is quite versatile (it'll double as sushi rice as well).

A GUIDE TO NUT-BASED SAUCES, MILKS, AND MORE

It's nuts how versatile your plant-based eating can be when you incorporate nuts! You can use them to make milk, sauces, dressings, cream, and cheeses that taste even better than their dairy-based counterparts. Plus, they're healthier because they're made from plants. I tend to rely on cashews because they're the most versatile, as well as neutral in flavor and relatively soft, which means they require less soaking time. However, if you're allergic to cashews or want to try something different, almonds, oats, soybeans, and pecans can all be made into nondairy milks easily at home.

How to Soak Cashews

For recipes using cashews in sauces, you'll generally need to soak them beforehand. However, **if you have a high-speed blender (such as a Vitamix or Blendtec), there is no need to soak them**—the blades of the blender are powerful enough to pulverize the cashews into a smooth sauce without this extra step.

For any recipe that transforms cashews into some sort of creamy substance, follow these basic instructions:

1. Depending on the recipe, begin with either whole cashews or cashew pieces. If you need to substitute one for the other, keep in mind that cashew pieces take up less space in the measuring cup, meaning you will need a little less than 1 cup of cashew pieces (about 2 tablespoons less) to equal the same amount as 1 cup whole cashews. **Always be sure to use unsalted, raw cashews** (not roasted and salted ones).

2. In a small bowl, soak the cashews in enough water to cover them for 2 to 4 hours. This will soften the cashews so they blend more easily.

3. Drain the nuts and use them as the recipe instructs.

- Amaranth
- Brown rice
- Buckwheat
- Millet
- Polenta
- Popcorn
- Quinoa
- Rolled oats

NUTS AND SEEDS

I recommend keeping a stock of the following nuts in a cool, dry cupboard (or refrigerator for extra freshness). *Be sure to buy these unsalted.*

- Almonds
- Cashews
- Chia seeds
- Peanuts, dry roasted
- Pecans

- Sesame seeds
- Sunflower seeds
- Walnuts

PASTA AND NOODLES

I have some excellent news for you—noodles are absolutely part of a healthy plant-based diet. The distinction lies in the type of noodle you choose. I avoid noodles that consist of refined flours, as they're stripped of nutrients and fiber. However, there are loads of great varieties that pass the healthy vegan test. I recommend:

- Bean-based pastas, such as the lentil lasagna noodles from Explore Cuisine
- Bean thread noodles (found in Asian markets and many grocery stores)
- Brown rice and millet ramen
- Brown rice linguine or capellini (Jovial is a great brand)
- Brown rice pad thai noodles
- Brown rice or quinoa spirals

DRIED HERBS AND SPICES

These ingredients stock my pantry and appear in my everyday cooking.

Basil: Essential for Italian dishes.

Black pepper: I recommend a medium grind for its versatility.

Cinnamon: Not just for baking, cinnamon also appears in many savory dishes.

Coriander: This is actually dried, powdered cilantro seed, although you wouldn't know that by tasting it.

Cumin, both ground and seeds: These are great for Mexican and Indian dishes.

Dill: You might think of it in relation to pickles, but dill complements a variety of tofu and potato dishes, too.

Garlic granules: Also known as granulated garlic, this is a more pleasant-tasting version of garlic powder. Garlic granules are often mislabeled as garlic powder, so look for the version that has a granulated (instead of powdery) appearance.

Nutmeg: You'll want to use pre-ground nutmeg, unless you're fancy and want to grate it yourself.

Onion granules: Like with garlic, onion granules are the better-tasting version of onion powder. They've got the same packaging problems as garlic granules, so keep your eyes peeled in the store.

Oregano: A classic Italian seasoning that pairs nicely with basil and garlic.

Red pepper flakes: I love using red pepper flakes to add a spicy, colorful kick to Asian dishes and sauces. It's also a must sprinkled on pizza.

Rosemary: Dried rosemary leaf is a fragrant addition to many dishes.

Turmeric: This is the ground, powdered root of the turmeric plant. It's got a strong earthy flavor and is very high in antioxidants and anti-inflammatory properties.

JARRED/BOTTLED PRODUCTS

I use oils in moderation, but the vinegars and sauces in this list will bring lots of flavor without added fats. I recommend keeping the following in your pantry rotation to amp up your cooking:

- Apple cider vinegar
- Balsamic vinegar
- Coconut aminos
- Cooking spray (such as coconut or avocado oil)
- Neutral-flavored oil (such as sunflower, avocado, or non-toasted sesame)
- Tamari (or shoyu)
- Toasted sesame oil
- Vegan marinara sauce

FLOURS

I suggest avoiding fiber-depleted white flour (also known as "unbleached wheat flour") in your kitchen. Look for the word "whole" when shopping for whole-grain flours, or go for bean or rice flours. I keep a few types on hand at all times, including:

- Brown rice flour
- Buckwheat flour
- Chickpea (garbanzo) flour
- Cornmeal
- Whole-wheat pastry flour

SWEETENERS

White sugar is something I suggest avoiding if possible, as it's a high-glycemic sweetener that can have inflammatory effects on the body. It's also sometimes bleached with animal bone char, unless it's organic. Some great natural alternatives include:

- Agave nectar
- Brown rice syrup
- Coconut sugar
- Maple syrup

UNCOMMON INGREDIENTS

Ah, the fun part! These unusual items may be new to you, but you don't want to go without them.

Nutritional yeast: a.k.a. the manna of vegan heaven. This flaky or powdery substance is actually just deactivated yeast, but it's high in B-vitamins and essential for making vegan cheeses and other items (it's also great sprinkled on popcorn, rice, and pasta). You can find it in many grocery stores these days and often in bulk at health food stores.

Cacao powder and cacao nibs: the least refined, nutrient-dense versions of chocolate.

Umeboshi vinegar: which comes from pickled ume plums (a Japanese fruit), is delicious in salads (see page 90). It's also much less expensive than its cousin, umeboshi paste. Find it in the Asian foods section of supermarkets and health food stores.

HOW TO PRESS TOFU

Tofu has a lot of water in it, which can make certain dishes soggy if it's not pressed out. I'll admit, I'm kind of old school when it comes to pressing tofu. People are constantly telling me to try the tofu press, and perhaps they're right, but it's so easy to do it the old-fashioned way, of which I have two methods.

The "In a Hurry" Method: For this "cheat" method, I simply slice the tofu into ½-inch-thick slabs, lay them out in a single layer on a cutting board, and place paper towels or tea towels over the top. Then, I press down gently (yet firmly) with my hands to remove the excess moisture. Honestly, I use this method 75 percent of the time because it suffices for most things.

The "Take Your Time" Method: The other 25 percent of the time, I either really want my tofu to absorb a marinade properly or I'm trying to impress fancy-pants guests. Slice the tofu into ½-inch-thick slabs, lay them out in a single layer on top of a paper towel or tea towel, then place more paper towels or tea towels on top. Place a baking sheet or cutting board over the towels and weigh it down with something heavy, such as jars of beans or grains or jugs of water. Press the tofu for at least 30 minutes or up to several hours until ready to marinate or cook.

REFRIGERATOR

It goes without saying that a healthy vegan refrigerator should include plenty of fruits and veggies, but since there are seemingly endless options, I won't list them all here. Instead, this section will focus on refrigerated ingredients specific to vegan eating and the recipes in this book.

HERBS

I like to keep fresh cilantro on hand at all times because I use it in Mexican, Thai, and Indian dishes. It will store for up to a week, but I don't suggest prepping it in advance, as it will go bad much more quickly if washed and chopped. If you're a big fan of fresh spring rolls (like I am), I also suggest keeping fresh basil and mint around.

NONDAIRY MILK

When I first went vegan in 1991, I remember only having about three kinds of nondairy milk to choose from—and none of them were in the refrigerator section. These days, there are so many options it can be overwhelming. I personally love oat milk for its delicious, creamy flavor and texture (Oatly is my favorite brand). However, I also use almond milk, as long as it's organic and unsweetened. You can also try cashew milk, pea milk, macadamia milk, rice milk (although that can be a bit thin), flax milk, and good old soy milk. Experiment to find your favorite, and if possible, opt for an unsweetened, plain variety—that will give you the most versatility.

TOFU

Tofu (a.k.a. bean curd) is a high-protein vegan staple that's made from soy milk. It's slightly more processed than tempeh or other whole foods, but is still a nutritious part of a plant-based diet. There are a myriad of varieties out there, but I primarily use two kinds. The first is water-packed, extra-firm tofu, found in the refrigerated section of health food stores and supermarkets. It's ideal for savory dishes, Everything Tofu (page 212), and sandwiches. The second kind is silken tofu (I always use firm), found in shelf-stable packs, and isn't necessary to refrigerate. It's a great base for salad dressings, Fresh Pumpkin Pie (page 186), and sauces.

TEMPEH

Tempeh is a minimally processed vegan protein made from soy (and possibly other grains, depending on the variety). It's high in fiber, iron, and protein. Because it's a fermented product, it's also good for digestion. Use tempeh in wraps like the Chicky Tempeh Wraps (page 117), or as an alternative to tofu. As with tofu, you'll want to infuse tempeh with flavor, because it's a bit bland on its own. Steaming it before seasoning helps it absorb flavor.

MISO PASTE

There are a few uncommon ingredients I can't live without, and at the top of that list is miso paste. It's made from fermented soybeans and is available in the refrigerated section of health food stores and most grocery stores. It's satisfyingly salty and gives an umami flavor to savory sauces, dressings, and soups. I recommend keeping both a light (or white) miso and a dark (or red) version on hand.

What You Won't Find Here: Processed Vegan Foods

Seitan: Although I'm not anti-seitan, I also don't include it in my cookbooks for a few reasons. Even though it's a good concentrated protein source (especially for soy-free vegans), it's also highly processed. Additionally, it's made from wheat, and I've come to include less of that (especially the refined type of wheat) in my diet over the years. I tend to think of seitan as a "treat" food to eat occasionally, rather than a regular part of my plant-based diet.

Packaged meat and dairy replacements: You can find tasty vegan alternatives to practically anything these days, but as with non-vegan foods, processed items that include lots of additives aren't ideal for your health. Since it's more than possible to make satisfying, delicious dishes from whole foods, processed products aren't necessary, so I haven't included them in this book. However, they can be extremely helpful for those transitioning to a vegan diet. My best advice is to enjoy them occasionally (if at all) and emphasize plant-strong foods for the most part.

BEANS, BEANS, THE MAGICAL FRUIT

The more you eat them . . . well, you know the rest. If you're worried about the, *ahem*, toot-factor of beans, I have good news for you—you can protect against it. If you're making beans from scratch, throw a small piece of kombu (a dried sea vegetable) into your cooking water and discard it once the beans are tender. It'll increase the beans' nutrients, as well as improve their digestibility. It's also imperative to cook your beans all the way through. I've occasionally bought brands of canned beans that aren't cooked enough, hence my recommendation for quality canned beans (such as Eden brand). The last line of defense against flatulence is rinsing your beans very well after soaking them, which reduces their gas-producing natural sugars.

ESSENTIAL TECHNIQUES

Beans and grains are a key part of your healthy vegan diet and a great source of protein, iron, calcium, and fiber. Knowing how to cook them properly is absolutely foundational. Refer to this section anytime the recipes call for cooked beans or grains.

HOW TO MAKE BEANS

Beans are humble little rock stars, let me tell you. They're inexpensive, unassuming, nutrient-dense, and unbelievably versatile. They make a great base for cheese (yes, cheese!) in the Low-Fat Cheese Dip (page 208) and even gravy in the Eat-It-Every-Day Gravy (page 211). I've even used them as a base for a chocolate dessert. Beans are also helpful for maintaining a healthy weight, as they're filling, yet low in calories. Follow the same cooking instructions regardless of the type of bean you're making:

1. In a pot, cover the beans in water and soak for 8 hours or overnight.

2. Pour out the soaking water and rinse the beans well. Return the beans to the pot.

3. Add the cooking water (see table), bring to a boil, then reduce the heat and simmer for 1½ to 2 hours, or until very tender.

4. Pour off any excess water and use in the recipe as directed.

The following table offers a handy guide for cooking a variety of beans:

TYPE OF BEAN (1 CUP DRY)	WATER	YIELD	BEST IN
Black beans	4 cups	2¼ cups	Mexican dishes, chili, black bean salads, brownies
Black-eyed peas	3 cups	2 cups	Tacos, with rice and kale, Southern dishes
Butter beans	4 cups	2 to 3 cups	Soups, stews, succotash, dips, salads
Cannellini beans (white kidney beans)	3 cups	2½ cups	Soups, salads, sautéed dishes, dips
Chickpeas	4 cups	2 cups	Hummus, Indian curries, salads, stir-fries
Great Northern beans (white beans)	3½ cups	2⅔ cups	Soups, salads, chilis
Kidney beans	3 cups	2¼ cups	Soups, chilis, salads, dips
Navy beans	4 cups	2⅔ cups	Dips, Italian salads, soups
Pinto beans	4 cups	2¾ cups	Mexican dishes, chili, soups, as the base for refried beans

HOW TO MAKE LENTILS

Lentils are a quicker-cooking type of "bean" and all-around versatile ingredient. I tend to rely on three varieties (red, yellow, and brown), but you can experiment with others such as green, black beluga, and Le Puy. Like beans, you should wash lentils well before cooking, but you don't need to soak them first. Simply bring them to a boil with water (see table below) and simmer until tender.

TYPE OF LENTIL (1 CUP DRY)	WATER	COOK FOR	YIELD	BEST IN
Brown	2½ cups	20 to 30 minutes	2¼ cups	Hearty soups, and alongside brown rice as an entrée
Red	3 cups	20 to 25 minutes	2½ cups	Chunky or blended soups, as they become very soft during cooking
Yellow	3 cups	30 to 40 minutes	2½ cups	Indian curries and soups

HOW TO MAKE GRAINS

Although there are many proponents of grain-free eating out there, I have to respectfully disagree. Whole grains are energy-giving, fiber-filled, nutrient-dense, and extremely satisfying. Below are the types you'll find in this book. No matter which variety you're cooking, follow these instructions:

1. In a heavy pot with a tight-fitting lid, bring grains and water (see table) to a boil, covered, over high heat.

2. Reduce the heat to low and simmer gently, still covered, until all the water has been absorbed and the grains are tender.

3. Remove lid and gently fluff with a fork.

TYPE OF GRAIN (1 CUP DRY)	WATER	COOK FOR	YIELD	BEST IN
Amaranth	2½ cups	20 to 25 minutes	2½ cups	Porridge, Popped Amaranth (page 60), breading
Buckwheat	2 cups	20 minutes	4 cups	Fillings, granola, cereals
Millet	3 cups	20 to 25 minutes	4 cups	Stand-in for rice, soups, stews
Oats (Rolled)	2 cups	5 to 10 minutes	3 cups	Desserts, oatmeal, granola
Quinoa	2 cups	12 to 15 minutes	3 cups	Salads, stand-in for rice
Short-Grain Brown Rice	2½ cups	40 to 45 minutes	3 cups	Sushi, stir-fries, fried rice, Simple Staple Rice (page 134)

LABELS YOU'LL SEE

You'll find the following labels at the top of each recipe (as they apply) to help you prep and plan.

○ **30 MINUTES OR LESS:** From start to finish, this recipe will take no more than 30 minutes.

◉ **GLUTEN-FREE:** The ingredients in this recipe do not contain any gluten.

● **LEFTOVER FRIENDLY:** This recipe stores well in the refrigerator or freezer and maintains its texture after being reheated (if reheating is necessary).

○ **NUT-FREE:** The ingredients in this recipe do not contain any nuts.

◉ **PLAN AHEAD:** This recipe requires ingredients that need to be prepared in advance, such as soaked nuts or cooked rice. *The prep and cook times for recipes with this label do not include the time it takes to prepare the plan-ahead ingredients.*

○ **WFPB:** This recipe adheres to a strict definition of the whole-foods, plant-based diet (no salt, oil, or refined sugar).

Anti-Inflammatory Tonic, page 22

CHAPTER THREE

SMOOTHIES, JUICES, AND SHAKES

ANTI-INFLAMMATORY TONIC

MAKES 5 TO 6 CUPS

Prep Time: 10 minutes

- ○ 30 MINUTES OR LESS
- ◑ GLUTEN-FREE
- ● LEFTOVER-FRIENDLY
- ○ NUT-FREE
- ○ WFPB

1 pineapple, peeled and cut into large chunks

8 ounces to 1 pound fresh ginger root (2 to 5 cups chopped)

1 ounce fresh turmeric root (about ¼ cup chopped)

1 lemon, quartered

¼ teaspoon freshly ground black pepper

There's something about taking a swig of this spicy, invigorating tonic that makes you feel invincible. The turmeric and ginger provide anti-inflammatory benefits, and the pineapple gives a nutritious, balancing sweetness, which prevents the need for additional sweeteners. The black pepper even boosts the nutritional properties of the turmeric. I personally prefer the full pound of ginger, but it's quite spicy that way. I'd suggest starting out with the half pound and adding more to taste, unless you're a spicy ginger maniac like me (and if you are, let's party). Please note that this makes a *lot* of tonic, but you can easily cut the recipe in half if you prefer.

1. If you have a juicer, cut the unpeeled pineapple into about 6 large chunks and run it through your juicer, along with the ginger, turmeric, and lemon. Stir in the black pepper. There will be a bit of foam on top, but that will eventually settle.

2. If using a blender, combine the pineapple, ginger, turmeric, lemon, and pepper in the blender and blend well. Over a large bowl, pour the mixture through cheesecloth or a fine-mesh sieve to strain. Squeeze out the excess juice from the pulp.

3. Refrigerate in an airtight container for up to 2 weeks, although the sooner you drink it, the better, as the nutritional benefits are highest within the first few days.

First-timer tip: There's no need to peel any of the produce if you're using a juicer. If you're using a blender, you'll want to peel the pineapple, but the other ingredients can remain whole.

Per serving (¼ cup): Calories: 125; Fat: 0g; Carbohydrates: 221g; Fiber: 13g; Protein: 2g; Sodium: 9mg; Iron: 1mg

SUPERFOOD SPRITZER

SERVES 1

Prep Time: 5 minutes

- ◯ 30 MINUTES OR LESS
- ◒ GLUTEN-FREE
- ● LEFTOVER-FRIENDLY
- ◯ NUT-FREE
- ◯ WFPB

FOR THE GOJI CONCENTRATE

2 cups water

½ cup dried goji berries

FOR THE SPRITZER

3 tablespoons goji concentrate

3 tablespoons freshly squeezed lemon juice

¼ teaspoon plain liquid stevia

1½ cups sparkling water

I drink this almost daily, and it never fails to make me feel revived. This tart, nutrient-dense drink is full of beta-carotene, vitamin C, and antioxidants, and is a great way to alkalinize your system. Plus, it's such a pretty color. I find myself reaching for this spritzer at night when I need a little "something" but don't want to compromise my healthy eating.

TO MAKE THE GOJI CONCENTRATE

In a blender, combine the water and goji berries, and blend until as smooth as possible. If you don't have a high-speed blender, you may want to use a fine-mesh strainer to remove any remaining pulp after you're done. This concentrate will keep for at least a week, refrigerated in an airtight container.

TO MAKE THE SPRITZER

In a tall glass, pour the goji concentrate, lemon juice, and stevia, then top with sparkling water. Stir and enjoy immediately.

———————————

Batch cooking tip: Since I'm way too into this drink, I make the goji concentrate by the double batch and keep it on hand. I also pre-squeeze my lemons so I always have fresh juice around. This way, it takes less than a minute to put together.

Per serving: Calories: 391; Fat: 0g; Carbohydrates: 88g; Fiber: 14g; Protein: 14g; Sodium: 299mg; Iron: 7mg

PINK POWER JUICE

SERVES 2

Prep Time: 5 minutes

○ 30 MINUTES OR LESS
● GLUTEN-FREE
○ NUT-FREE
○ WFPB

1 large beet, peeled and chopped

4 large carrots, quartered

2-inch piece fresh ginger

Juice of 1½ lemons

1 small bunch fresh parsley or cilantro

There's nothing like a fresh vegetable juice to rev up your immune system, give you a boost of energy, and make you feel like you can take on the day. Pink is an understatement for this vibrantly colored juice, which is also rich in iron, beta-carotene, chlorophyll, and the anti-inflammatory benefits of ginger. Speaking of which, my family is full of ginger fiends, so I actually use more ginger than this recipe calls for when I make this juice, but this is a good amount for an "I like ginger" type of person. Feel free to adjust the amount to your liking.

1. In a blender, combine the beet, carrots, ginger, lemon juice, and parsley. Blend until completely smooth.

2. Over a large bowl, pour the mixture through cheesecloth or a fine-mesh sieve to strain the juice. Squeeze out the excess juice from the pulp. Drink immediately for maximum nutritional benefits.

———————————

Variation tip: If you've got a juicer, there's no need to peel anything. You can juice all of the "ugly" parts of a beet, the stems of greens, the ends of carrots, and even throw that lemon in whole. Any good juicer will separate all of the unwanted portions, so all you're left with is divinely delicious juice.

Per serving: Calories: 86; Fat: 1g; Carbohydrates: 21g; Fiber: 5g; Protein: 2g; Sodium: 132mg; Iron: 1mg

ELECTROLYTE ME UP SMOOTHIE

SERVES 2 TO 4

Prep Time: 5 minutes

- ○ 30 MINUTES OR LESS
- ◉ GLUTEN-FREE
- ○ NUT-FREE
- ○ WFPB

3 cups frozen pineapple chunks

2 cups coconut water

2 cups firmly packed chopped kale

2 medium celery stalks, leaves removed (1 cup chopped)

¼ cup freshly squeezed lime juice

This smoothie really will light you up, with a plant-strong electrolyte boost, that is. I always feel great when I drink this, because I'm getting in lots of greens, alkaline foods, and of course, those magical electrolytes. If you're new to green smoothies, feel free to begin with half the kale and work your way up—I like a power punch of greens, but some people like their smoothies a little sweeter. This is great for breakfast or as a pick-me-up any time of day.

In a blender, combine the pineapple, coconut water, kale, celery, and lime juice and process until completely smooth. Serve immediately.

First-timer tip: If you're not using a high-speed blender (such as a Vitamix or Blendtec), you may wish to use baby kale or spinach instead of regular kale. You may also want to cut the celery up into small pieces so that it blends properly. You can use either fresh or refrigerated coconut water here, although fresh (from young Thai coconuts) is unbeatable.

Per serving: Calories: 88; Fat: 0g; Carbohydrates: 22g; Fiber: 2g; Protein: 1g; Sodium: 25mg; Iron: 1mg

GO GREEN JUICE

SERVES 2

Prep Time: 5 minutes

○ 30 MINUTES OR LESS
◐ GLUTEN-FREE
○ NUT-FREE
○ WFPB

1 large cucumber, quartered

3 cups diced pineapple (optional)

3 celery stalks, quartered

1 large handful kale

1 small bunch fresh cilantro

Juice of 2 limes

1 small jalapeño (optional)

This powerhouse of a drink will leave you feeling fantastic—and yes, ready to go, go, go! I often prefer a veggies-only juice, so I frequently make up a version without the pineapple. Customize it however you like. I trust you.

1. In a blender, combine the cucumber, pineapple (if using), celery, kale, cilantro, lime juice, and jalapeño (if using) and blend well until completely smooth.

2. Over a large bowl, pour the mixture through cheesecloth or a fine-mesh sieve to strain the juice. Squeeze out the excess juice from the pulp. Drink immediately for maximum nutritional benefits.

Substitution tip: You can substitute any greens for the kale and cilantro. Some of my favorites to use in this juice include parsley, spinach, and chard.

Variation tip: Use a juicer instead and don't bother juicing those limes beforehand or cutting anything (except the pineapple—that probably won't fit in your juicer whole).

Per serving: Calories: 58; Fat: 1g; Carbohydrates: 12g; Fiber: 5g; Protein: 3g; Sodium: 1mg; Iron: 0mg

STRAWBERRY MYLK

SERVES 6

Prep Time: 5 minutes

- ○ GLUTEN-FREE
- ● LEFTOVER-FRIENDLY
- ○ PLAN AHEAD

1½ cups water

½ cup raw unsalted whole cashews, soaked, drained, and rinsed (see page 11)

½ cup pitted dates (about 5 large dates)

1 cup strawberries, fresh or frozen

1 teaspoon vanilla extract

⅛ teaspoon sea salt

If heavenly nectar was an actual thing, this would be the recipe. This silky-smooth, luscious plant-based mylk is delectable and works well as a mini-meal, dessert, snack, or breakfast when poured over Buckwheat Crisps (page 199). Dates add the perfect amount of sweetness here, with the added benefits of fiber and iron.

1. In a blender, combine 1½ cups of water, cashews, and dates. Process very well, until completely smooth.

2. Add the strawberries, vanilla, and salt, and blend until velvety smooth. Refrigerate in an airtight container for up to week.

_____

First-timer tip: Even if you buy pitted dates, be sure to double-check that they are all, in fact, pitted. Once in a while, a pit will slip through the packaging process and end up in your bag of "pitted" dates. If you accidentally blend one up, it could ruin your mylk, and you don't need that sort of negativity in your life.

Per serving: Calories: 88; Fat: 5g; Carbohydrates: 9g; Fiber: 1g; Protein: 4g; Sodium: 13mg; Iron: 1mg

CHOCOLATE MYLK

SERVES 12

Prep Time: 5 minutes

- GLUTEN-FREE
- LEFTOVER-FRIENDLY
- PLAN AHEAD

2 cups water

1 cup raw unsalted whole cashews, soaked, drained, and rinsed (see page 11)

1 cup pitted dates (12 large dates)

½ cup raw cacao powder

2 tablespoons maple syrup

1 tablespoon vanilla extract

¾ teaspoon sea salt

Most of us associate chocolate milk with something unhealthy and decadent, but my superfood twist on this classic drink is actually good for you. The antioxidants in raw cacao powder give you the very best of what chocolate has to offer in its purest form, and it can be found at any health food store. This mylk is mostly sweetened with dates, which makes this one of the most wholesome treats in town. You can feel great about indulging in this deliciousness.

1. In a blender, combine 2 cups of water, cashews, dates, and cacao. Process until completely smooth.

2. Add the maple syrup, vanilla, and salt and blend until velvety smooth. Refrigerate in an airtight container for up to 10 days.

Variation tip: To make this even more nutrient-dense, add 2 to 3 tablespoons of performance mushroom (yes, mushroom!) powder. The one I use (Laird Superfood brand) has a blend of chaga, cordyceps, lion's mane, and maitake, which have been valued in Eastern medicine for hundreds of years. You can't taste any mushroomy-ness, but it does give the drink an umami flavor, enriching the depth of the chocolate even more. Talk about a win-win!

Variation tip: For chocolate-mint mylk, add 1 teaspoon peppermint flavoring. Easy peasy, and absolutely, positively delicious.

Variation tip: For hot chocolate, simply heat in a saucepan over low heat for a few minutes, until warmed through.

Per serving: Calories: 136; Fat: 7g; Carbohydrates: 15g; Fiber: 2g; Protein: 6g; Sodium: 25mg; Iron: 6mg

VANILLA MYLKSHAKE

SERVES 1 TO 2

Prep Time: 2 minutes

- GLUTEN-FREE
- PLAN AHEAD
- WFPB

½ cup raw unsalted whole cashews, soaked, drained, and rinsed (see page 11)

2 ripe peeled bananas, broken into chunks and frozen

1 teaspoon vanilla extract

1½ cups unsweetened plain or vanilla nondairy milk, divided

This creamy shake is the height of healthy simplicity. I make this several times a week for my daughter to help her get in sustaining, healthy calories before a long day of school. If you're not used to freezing bananas, be sure to choose ones that are very ripe, and peel them before popping them into a plastic bag in the freezer. Once they've been in there overnight, they're ready to party.

In a blender, combine the cashews, bananas, vanilla, and just enough of the milk to blend, about ½ cup. Process until as smooth as possible, then blend in the remaining 1 cup milk. Serve immediately.

Variation tip: If you prefer your shake a little sweeter, toss in a few pitted dates. You can also add a dash of salt if you'd like to make the flavor pop a bit more.

Per serving: Calories: 60; Fat: 15g; Carbohydrates: 38g; Fiber: 5g; Protein: 7g; Sodium: 138mg; Iron: 2mg

TROPICAL GREEN SMOOTHIE

SERVES 4

Prep Time: 5 minutes

- ○ 30 MINUTES OR LESS
- ● GLUTEN-FREE
- ○ NUT-FREE
- ● PLAN AHEAD
- ○ WFPB

4 cups packed spinach

2 cups frozen pineapple chunks

2 cups frozen mango chunks

1¾ cups orange juice

1 cup unsweetened plain nondairy yogurt

1 ripe peeled banana, broken into chunks and frozen

This is my daughter's go-to smoothie, although she'll tell you to add strawberries. I prefer the simpler combination below, but if you want to try her suggestion, use half strawberries and half mango. To ensure a nice, thick smoothie from the get-go, be sure your fruit is fully frozen and start with the minimum amount of juice, only adding more as needed. We love to use So Delicious Dairy Free brand coconut yogurt for this recipe because it's unsweetened and so tangy.

In a blender, combine the spinach, pineapple, mango, orange juice, yogurt, and banana and blend until all of the ingredients are thoroughly emulsified. If necessary, add slightly more orange juice or water. If your mixture is too thin, add more frozen fruit. Drink immediately.

——————————

Variation tip: This mixture makes great popsicles. Pour the smoothie base into popsicle molds and freeze until solid. You can also add chunks of whole fruit to the base for added fun.

Per serving: Calories: 197; Fat: 3g; Carbohydrates: 44g; Fiber: 5g; Protein: 4g; Sodium: 41mg; Iron: 2mg

WATERMELON LIME COOLER

SERVES 5

Prep Time: 5 minutes

- ○ 30 MINUTES OR LESS
- ◑ GLUTEN-FREE
- ● LEFTOVER-FRIENDLY
- ○ NUT-FREE
- ○ WFPB

6 cups chopped watermelon

2 cups frozen strawberries

½ cup freshly squeezed lime juice

Oh, how I love this drink. To me, it's summer in a glass—refreshing, satisfying, and made from only whole foods. You're getting all the nutrients and fiber of whole, fresh strawberries and watermelon, along with the alkalinizing benefits and tang of lime, in a way that's easy to enjoy, even on the go.

In a blender, combine the watermelon, strawberries, and lime juice and blend until smooth. Serve cold. Refrigerate in an airtight container for up to a week.

———————————

Variation tip: The sweetness of watermelon and strawberries can really vary depending on the season. If yours are both on the sweet side, this drink will be perfect as is. If they're a little tart, you may wish to add less lime juice, some extra strawberries, or a squeeze of liquid stevia.

Per serving: Calories: 82; Fat: 0g; Carbohydrates: 21g; Fiber: 2g; Protein: 2g; Sodium: 2mg; Iron: 1mg

BLUEBERRY SUPERFOOD PROTEIN SHAKE

SERVES 4 (OR 1 TO 2 AS A MEAL)

Prep Time: 5 minutes

- ○ 30 MINUTES OR LESS
- ● GLUTEN-FREE
- ○ NUT-FREE
- ● PLAN AHEAD
- ○ WFPB

2 cups frozen blueberries

1½ cups unsweetened nondairy milk

1 ripe peeled banana, broken into chunks and frozen

1 very large handful fresh spinach

½ cup cooked chickpeas (see page 17)

4 pitted dates

2 tablespoons chia seeds

I find myself relying on this recipe on a regular basis, because it's seriously supercharging. This drink will boost your energy and provide loads of antioxidants, fiber, and vitamins. It's also incredibly quick to make, with ingredients that are easy to keep on hand at all times. When I'm on the go, I blend up a batch of this and it keeps me going happily until my next meal.

In a blender, combine the blueberries, milk, banana, spinach, chickpeas, dates, and chia seeds and process until completely smooth. Serve immediately.

———————————

Fun fact: The first time I made this was on Halloween, when I found out at the last minute that I had to drive my daughter all over creation. I was pretty hungry but didn't want to be tempted to eat out. So, I threw a bunch of satisfying, nutrient-dense ingredients in the blender and it kept me going until the next morning. I hope this recipe will save you from impending doom sometime, too.

Per serving: Calories: 253; Fat: 7g; Carbohydrates: 37g; Fiber: 16g; Protein: 6g; Sodium: 106mg; Iron: 2mg

TURMERIC GODDESS SHAKE

SERVES 2 TO 4

Prep Time: 5 minutes

- ○ 30 MINUTES OR LESS
- ◉ GLUTEN-FREE
- ○ NUT-FREE
- ◉ PLAN AHEAD
- ○ WFPB

4 ripe peeled bananas, broken into chunks and frozen

2 cups unsweetened oat milk

¼ cup coconut butter

6 large pitted dates

1 tablespoon ground turmeric

¼ teaspoon freshly ground black pepper

This nutrient-dense, anti-inflammatory elixir is easy to make and absolutely delicious. I generally prefer it just as is, but it's also wonderful with the "ginger spice" variation in the tip below. You can even add ginger to the basic recipe for a ginger-turmeric shake. No matter what, your taste buds will love this, and so will your body.

In a blender, combine the bananas, oat milk, coconut butter, dates, turmeric, and pepper, and process until completely smooth. Serve immediately.

Ingredient tip: Coconut butter is simply the purée of coconut meat, and it is absolutely divine. Find it in any health food store or online, or substitute almond butter if needed.

Variation tip: For a Ginger Spice Goddess Shake, blend the following along with the original ingredients: 2 tablespoons grated fresh ginger, ½ teaspoon ground cinnamon, and ¼ teaspoon ground nutmeg.

Per serving: Calories: 646; Fat: 43g; Carbohydrates: 59g; Fiber: 13g; Protein: 10g; Sodium: 107mg; Iron: 6mg

VEGAN EGGNOG

SERVES 6

Prep Time: 5 minutes

- ● GLUTEN-FREE
- ● LEFTOVER-FRIENDLY
- ● PLAN AHEAD

1 ripe peeled fresh or frozen banana

¼ cup raw unsalted cashew pieces, soaked, drained, and rinsed (see page 11)

2 cups unsweetened nondairy milk, divided

¼ cup maple syrup

1 tablespoon vanilla extract

½ teaspoon ground nutmeg, plus more for garnish

⅛ teaspoon sea salt

⅛ teaspoon ground cinnamon

This creamy, luscious, delectable eggnog has won over more omnivores than I can even remember. People are usually surprised when I tell them this is not only vegan, but healthy! So healthy, in fact, that you can drink it for breakfast and still feel like a total adult. This eggnog is perfect for the holidays, but easy and nutritious enough to enjoy any time of year. It also happens to be one of my (picky, but wonderful) daughter's all-time favorite drinks. If you love it even half as much as she does, my work here is done.

1. In a blender, combine the banana, cashews, and just enough of the milk to blend, about ½ cup. Process until creamy, then add the remaining 1½ cups milk, maple syrup, vanilla, nutmeg, salt, and cinnamon. Blend until completely smooth.

2. Serve with a little extra nutmeg sprinkled on top. Refrigerate in an airtight container for up to 3 days.

Substitution tip: What if you're dying to make this and have everything on hand—except the milk? Never fear. Just add in an extra handful of cashews and use water instead of milk.

Per serving: Calories: 108; Fat: 4g; Carbohydrates: 16g; Fiber: 1g; Protein: 2g; Sodium: 62mg; Iron: 1mg

Pretty Pitaya Bowl, page 43

BREAKFAST

SUPERFOOD GRANOLA

MAKES ABOUT 6 CUPS

Prep Time: 15 minutes
Cook Time: 2½ hours

○ GLUTEN-FREE
● LEFTOVER-FRIENDLY
○ PLAN AHEAD

1 cup millet, soaked for 8 to 12 hours

1½ cups firmly packed raisins

1 cup raw unsalted walnuts

½ cup water

¼ cup chia seeds

1 tablespoon vanilla extract

½ teaspoon sea salt

3½ cups rolled oats

¼ cup maple syrup

Variation tip: You can also use a dehydrator instead of baking the granola. Lay the granola in a single layer on your dehydrator sheets (I use four large trays in my Excalibur dehydrator). Dehydrate at 105°F for 6 to 7 hours, or until no moisture remains and it seems "cooked." For a spiced twist, add 1 tablespoon ground cinnamon and ¼ teaspoon ground nutmeg to the mix, along with the water in step 2, before baking or dehydrating it.

Per serving (½ cup): Calories: 283; Fat: 9g; Carbohydrates: 46g; Fiber: 6g; Protein: 7g; Sodium: 1mg; Iron: 2mg

I used to avoid granola because, although it's delicious, it always seemed overly sweet and oily to me. However, this version is next-level healthy. It's a powerhouse of nutrient-dense yumminess you can eat plain, over berries with nondairy milk, or even as a dessert topping like in the Apple Crisp with Creamy Lemon Sauce (page 182). This recipe makes a big batch, but you'll be glad you have it on hand, as it will stay fresh for at least a month—although I've never been able to make it last that long in our house.

1. Preheat the oven to 200°F. Line two large baking sheets with silicone liners or parchment paper and set aside.

2. Drain and rinse the soaked millet and place in a food processor along with the raisins and walnuts. Process until well blended. Add the water, chia seeds, vanilla, and salt. Blend until there are no visible raisins or big chunks of walnuts, but the mixture still has some texture.

3. Transfer the mixture to a large bowl. Stir in the oats and maple syrup. (I actually use my hands for this. It's a great excuse to sneak a few tastes.)

4. Spread the granola out in a single layer on the prepared baking sheets. Bake for about 2½ hours, stirring once or twice during baking. It will crisp up a bit during cooling.

5. Once completely cooled, store at room temperature in an airtight container for up to 1 month.

TESS'S FAVORITE BREAKFAST BOWL

SERVES 1

Prep Time: 2 minutes

- GLUTEN-FREE
- PLAN AHEAD

¾ cup plain unsweetened nondairy yogurt

½ cup Superfood Granola (page 40)

½ cup berries of choice

Because we have a habit of keeping the Superfood Granola (page 40) on hand at our house, this breakfast bowl is my go-to. I love the way the tart, creamy coconut yogurt pairs with the slightly sweet, crunchy granola and the freshness of the berries. I also love knowing that I'm totally nourishing my body with this dish, because foods that are both nutritious and delicious are simply where it's at. This recipe serves one, but it's very easy to make a bigger batch if you're nice enough to share.

1. Place the yogurt in a bowl and top with the granola.

2. Sprinkle the berries on top and serve immediately. I especially love raspberries for this, but mixed berries are also nice.

Fun fact: This is one of my favorite road-trip foods because it's beyond easy to pack a big container of the Superfood Granola and throw some coconut yogurt and berries in the cooler. A nourishing, satisfying meal at my fingertips while I'm on the go? Yes, please.

Variation tip: For even more superfoodie-ness, sprinkle with a teaspoon each of chia seeds and hemp seeds before serving.

Per serving: Calories: 153; Fat: 7g; Carbohydrates: 21g; Fiber: 4g; Protein: 2g; Sodium: 40mg; Iron: 1mg

MEAL PREP CHIA BREAKFAST BOWL

SERVES 4

Prep Time: 2 minutes, plus
2 hours for chilling

- ● GLUTEN-FREE
- ● LEFTOVER-FRIENDLY
- ○ NUT-FREE
- ● PLAN AHEAD
- ○ WFPB

2 cups plain unsweetened almond or oat milk

½ cup chia seeds

3 tablespoons maple syrup

2 teaspoons vanilla extract

1 cup Buckwheat Crisps (page 199)

4 cups berries of choice

You may notice there's no "30 Minutes or Less" tag on this recipe, but don't let that deter you. The actual time you'll spend preparing the elements of this dish are very minimal—it's just a matter of waiting for the chia pudding to thicken and making sure to have the Buckwheat Crisps (page 199) on hand, making it perfect for all those meal preppers out there. I love this dish for on-the-go moments (not just around breakfast time), because it's satisfying, crunchy, and easy to eat. Plus, it gives me a great energy boost when I need it.

1. In a large airtight container, combine the milk, chia seeds, maple syrup, and vanilla. Stir well. Cover and refrigerate for about 2 hours, or until thick. You may need to stir or whisk intermittently, as the chia seeds can clump together.

2. Place the chia pudding in bowls and top with the Buckwheat Crisps and berries. Serve immediately.

Batch cooking tip: I like to have this on hand for my family to eat all week, so I make up a triple batch of the chia pudding and Buckwheat Crisps. Then, anytime someone needs a healthy breakfast or mini-meal, it takes less than a minute to put together. Refrigerate the chia pudding in an airtight container for up to a week.

Per serving: Calories: 348; Fat: 8g; Carbohydrates: 62g; Fiber: 14g; Protein: 9g; Sodium: 99mg; Iron: 4mg

PRETTY PITAYA BOWL

SERVES 2

Prep Time: 5 minutes

- ○ GLUTEN-FREE
- ○ PLAN AHEAD

1½ cups Superfood Granola (page 40)

1 (100-gram) packet frozen pitaya smoothie blend (pitaya pulp and seeds)

2 cups frozen raspberries

1 large ripe banana, frozen

1 cup orange juice

2 tablespoons coconut butter (puréed coconut)

1 teaspoon chia seeds

¾ cup sliced strawberries

This smoothie bowl is absolutely gorgeous, thanks to brilliant pink pitaya (a.k.a. dragon fruit). The raspberries also intensify the color and add the perfect amount of tang. If you like your smoothie bowls on the sweeter side, drizzle this with brown rice syrup or agave nectar. This bowl is the perfect reminder that you don't have to sacrifice anything to enjoy fabulous food—it's all at once pretty to look at, incredibly nourishing, and unbearably delicious.

1. Into each bowl, place ¼ cup of the granola and set aside.

2. In a blender or food processor, combine the pitaya, raspberries, banana, orange juice, and coconut butter. Blend until completely smooth. If needed, add more orange juice a tablespoon at a time, taking care to retain maximum thickness.

3. Divide the mixture evenly between the bowls, on top of the granola. Divide the remaining 1 cup granola between the bowls and sprinkle with chia seeds. Arrange the strawberries on top and serve immediately.

Make it WFPB: Omit the salt from the granola.

Ingredient tip: Pitaya may sound like an exotic ingredient, especially in frozen smoothie-blend form, but you can find this product in common stores like Target, Whole Foods, and just about any supermarket. Look for it in the frozen fruit section.

Per serving: Calories: 900; Fat: 48g; Carbohydrates: 112g; Fiber: 32g; Protein: 13g; Sodium: 24mg; Iron: 7mg

BLACKBERRY CHIA PUDDING

SERVES 6

Prep Time: 5 minutes, plus
2 hours for chilling

- GLUTEN-FREE
- LEFTOVER-FRIENDLY
- PLAN AHEAD
- WFPB

2 cups water

1 cup blackberries

¼ cup raw unsalted whole cashews, soaked, drained, and rinsed (see page 11)

2 tablespoons maple syrup

1 teaspoon vanilla extract

⅓ cup chia seeds

This pudding is simple, yet very tasty—the quintessential energy snack. Chia seeds are a great source of omega-3s, and the blackberries provide loads of antioxidants and fiber. Enjoy this plain or topped with additional berries.

1. In a blender, combine the water, blackberries, cashews, maple syrup, and vanilla and process until very smooth. Transfer to an airtight container.

2. Stir in the chia seeds and refrigerate, covered, for 2 hours, or until thickened. You may need to stir intermittently, as the chia seeds tend to clump together. Refrigerate in an airtight container for up to a week.

First-timer tip: If you're new to chia pudding, you'll be happy to know that it's extremely easy to throw together and modify. It's basically a superfood "instant pudding," and if you ever prefer a thicker version, you can simply add more chia.

Per serving: Calories: 100; Fat: 5g; Carbohydrates: 13g; Fiber: 5g; Protein: 2g; Sodium: 3mg; Iron: 1mg

BLUEBERRY LEMON CHEESECAKE OATMEAL

SERVES 4 TO 6

Prep Time: 10 minutes
Cook Time: 10 minutes

- GLUTEN-FREE
- PLAN AHEAD

FOR THE CREAMY LEMON SAUCE

1 cup raw unsalted cashew pieces, soaked, drained, and rinsed (see page 11)

½ cup maple syrup

¼ cup water

3 tablespoons freshly squeezed lemon juice

2 teaspoons lemon zest

2 tablespoons sunflower or avocado oil

2 teaspoons vanilla extract

¼ teaspoon sea salt

FOR THE OATMEAL

3½ cups water

1¾ cups rolled oats

1 cup blueberries

Although I typically find oatmeal boring, this twist is absolutely crave-worthy. For an extra treat, serve topped with Superfood Granola (page 40) or a few walnuts. If you'd like to take this to near-dessert status, you can even add a dollop of fruit-sweetened blueberry jam on top.

TO MAKE THE CREAMY LEMON SAUCE
In a blender, combine the cashews, maple syrup, water, lemon juice and zest, oil, vanilla, and salt and process until completely smooth and velvety.

TO MAKE THE OATMEAL
1. In a medium pot, bring the water and oats to a boil. Reduce the heat to low and simmer, stirring often, for 5 to 10 minutes, or until the oats are tender and the water has been absorbed.

2. Stir in the blueberries and let sit for a minute or two. Stir again, top with the creamy lemon sauce, and serve immediately.

Make it WFPB: Omit the oil and salt from the lemon sauce. If necessary, add an additional 2 tablespoons water as a replacement.

Per serving: Calories: 315; Fat: 15g; Carbohydrates: 43g; Fiber: 3g; Protein: 7g; Sodium: 4mg; Iron: 3mg

APPLE PIE POWERHOUSE PORRIDGE

SERVES 4

Prep Time: 5 minutes

Cook Time: 15 minutes

○ 30 MINUTES OR LESS
● GLUTEN-FREE
○ NUT-FREE

3½ cups water

1 cup rolled oats

1 large apple, finely chopped (1 cup)

¼ cup buckwheat

2 tablespoons amaranth

1 tablespoon chia seeds

2 tablespoons coconut sugar

2 teaspoons ground cinnamon

⅛ teaspoon ground nutmeg

Dash sea salt

This hot breakfast cereal will warm you up and make you feel like a champion. Amaranth is one of the world's most nutrient-dense foods, buckwheat is incredibly nourishing, and chia seeds provide yet another boost of antioxidants and omega-3s. If you ever need a quick meal that's as healthy as possible, this porridge does the trick. To really take this over the top, sprinkle with some Superfood Granola (page 40) before serving.

1. In a medium pot, combine the water, oats, apple, buckwheat, amaranth, chia seeds, coconut sugar, cinnamon, nutmeg, and salt over medium heat. Bring to a boil.

2. Reduce the heat to low and simmer, stirring often, for 10 to 15 minutes, or until all of the water has been absorbed. Remove from the heat. Serve immediately, plain or topped with nondairy milk and/or maple syrup.

Variation tip: For a *berry* different flavor (sorry, can't help myself sometimes), omit the cinnamon, nutmeg, and apple. Once cooked, stir in a cup of blueberries, strawberries, raspberries, or blackberries.

Per serving: Calories: 195; Fat: 3g; Carbohydrates: 39g; Fiber: 6g; Protein: 5g; Sodium: 1mg; Iron: 1mg

AVOCADO TOAST WITH CHIPOTLE CREAM SAUCE

SERVES 3

Prep Time: 3 minutes
Cook Time: 1 to 2 minutes

○ GLUTEN-FREE
○ PLAN AHEAD

3 whole-grain or gluten-free bread slices

1 small avocado, halved and pitted

3 tablespoons Chipotle Cream Sauce (page 206)

¾ teaspoon nutritional yeast

2 teaspoons dried chipotle flakes

Whenever we're in Flagstaff or Sedona, we visit a place called Local Juicery, partly because they have the very best avocado toast. After becoming rightly obsessed with it, I decided to re-create it at home (minus the alfalfa sprouts they put on top), and I have to tell you—this recipe is about as close as it gets. I actually feel like I'm at their cute café when I eat it. For an extra-hearty breakfast, enjoy alongside some Savory Scrambled Tofu (page 49), a Pretty Pitaya Bowl (page 43), or a Tropical Green Smoothie (page 31). This toast also happens to make a great mini-meal any time of day.

1. Toast the bread slices, then lay them on plates.

2. Using a spoon, scoop out the flesh from the avocado and evenly distribute it onto the toast slices. Mash down with a fork.

3. Drizzle the chipotle sauce on top of the avocado. Sprinkle with nutritional yeast and top with the chipotle flakes. Serve immediately.

Ingredient tip: Chipotle flakes can be a little tricky to find, but the wonderful crunchy texture and rich, smoky flavor they provide are unmatched. After striking out at local stores, we bought ours on Amazon for a reasonable price. They're definitely worth the trouble, so don't skip them.

Make it WFPB: Omit the salt from the Chipotle Cream Sauce.

Per serving: Calories: 231; Fat: 12g; Carbohydrates: 26g; Fiber: 8g; Protein: 8g; Sodium: 165mg; Iron: 2mg

SAVORY SCRAMBLED TOFU

SERVES 4

Prep Time: 5 minutes
Cook Time: 10 minutes

- ○ 30 MINUTES OR LESS
- ◐ GLUTEN-FREE
- ● LEFTOVER-FRIENDLY
- ○ NUT-FREE

1 pound firm tofu

2 tablespoons sunflower or olive oil

1 teaspoon ground turmeric

¼ cup nutritional yeast

1 tablespoon tamari, shoyu, or soy sauce

3 medium garlic cloves, minced or pressed

2 teaspoons onion granules or powder

2 teaspoons dried dill

1 teaspoon dried rosemary

Sea salt

Freshly ground black pepper

If you've ever had bland tofu in restaurants, you'll appreciate this full-flavored dish. My daughter is so used to this version now that she simply won't eat scrambled tofu in restaurants—she's always too disappointed. The secret is plenty of spices and garlic—and a healthy dose of nutritional yeast. This makes for the perfect breakfast feast alongside some Blueberry-Banana Buckwheat Crunch Pancakes (page 57) and a Tropical Green Smoothie (page 31).

1. In a colander over the sink, crumble the tofu, squeezing out the excess water with your hands. Set aside.

2. In a large skillet or wok, heat the oil over medium-high heat. When it just begins to shimmer, add the tofu and turmeric and cook for 2 to 3 minutes, stirring often, until heated through.

3. Add the nutritional yeast, tamari, garlic, onion granules, dill, and rosemary. Stir well.

4. Continue to cook for 5 to 10 minutes, stirring often, until the tofu becomes golden brown and slightly crisp. Season with salt and pepper. Serve immediately. Refrigerate leftovers in an airtight container for up to 3 days.

Make it WFPB: Omit the oil and salt and use water to sauté the tofu.

Per serving: Calories: 193; Fat: 9g; Carbohydrates: 7g; Fiber: 3g; Protein: 14g; Sodium: 253mg; Iron: 2mg

10-MINUTE TACOS

SERVES 4

Prep Time: 5 minutes

Cook Time: 5 minutes

⬤ GLUTEN-FREE
⬤ LEFTOVER-FRIENDLY
◯ NUT-FREE
⬤ PLAN AHEAD

8 ounces firm tofu

1 (15-ounce) can pinto or black beans, drained and rinsed, or 1½ cups cooked pinto beans (see page 17)

½ carrot, grated

2 tablespoons nutritional yeast

¾ cup store-bought salsa or Classic Salsa (page 202), plus more for serving

4 to 8 corn tortillas (preferably sprouted)

½ cup Avotillo Sauce (page 201)

¼ cup Classic Guacamole (page 64)

¼ cup Low-Fat Cheese Dip (page 208)

These tacos are the essence of simplicity. Only 10 minutes from start to finish, though you can make the filling in advance for an even quicker breakfast on the go. To jazz them up, add one of the serving sauces—my family's favorite is the Avotillo Sauce (page 201) or some additional salsa paired with the Low-Fat Cheese Dip (page 208). These tacos are also delicious with roasted potatoes or grilled onions added in.

1. In a large skillet over medium-high heat, crumble the tofu. This recipe does not call for frying in oil, so no need to press out the excess water beforehand.

2. Add the beans, carrot, and nutritional yeast. Sauté for about 2 minutes, stirring occasionally. Add the salsa and cook another minute, or until warmed through.

3. While the tofu mixture is cooking, heat the tortillas. Especially for thicker (or sprouted) corn tortillas, I like to rinse them lightly with water and place them in a hot dry (or lightly oiled) pan for several seconds on each side, as that will soften and warm them.

4. To serve, fill each tortilla with the mixture and top with Avotillo Sauce, Classic Guacamole, and Low-Fat Cheese Dip. Enjoy immediately. If you have extra filling, refrigerate leftovers for up to a week in an airtight container.

Substitution tip: If you're soy-free or just don't feel the tofu love, you can omit it and use hash browns or extra beans instead. If you're using hash browns or diced potatoes, you'll need to sauté them for several minutes in water or vegetable broth until they're soft before adding the remaining ingredients. And then, of course, you'll need to change the name of this recipe, because they'll take longer than 10 minutes.

Per serving: Calories: 315; Fat: 8g; Carbohydrates: 43g; Fiber: 12g; Protein: 18g; Sodium: 357mg; Iron: 4mg

POTATO-KALE TAQUITOS

SERVES 4

Prep Time: 10 minutes
Cook Time: 35 minutes

○ GLUTEN-FREE
○ PLAN AHEAD

2 medium potatoes, peeled and finely diced (2½ cups)

1 cup finely chopped kale

¼ cup plain unsweetened nondairy milk

3 large garlic cloves, minced or pressed

½ teaspoon sea salt

¼ teaspoon freshly ground black pepper

¼ cup minced scallions, both white and green parts

8 corn tortillas (preferably sprouted)

½ cup Low-Fat Cheese Dip (page 208) or Chipotle Cream Sauce (page 206)

½ cup Classic Salsa (page 202) (optional)

Meal prep it: To plan ahead, make the cheese dip (and other sauces, if using) in advance, as they will last for up to a week. Then, make a batch (or double batch) of the potato-kale filling. It will keep, refrigerated in an airtight container, for up to a week as well. When it's time to make the taquitos, your actual prep time will only be about 2 minutes.

Per serving: Calories: 231; Fat: 6g; Carbohydrates: 40g; Fiber: 4g; Protein: 8g; Sodium: 19mg; Iron: 1mg

If you're a savory breakfast person like me, you'll love this dish. Creamy mashed potatoes paired with iron-rich kale, topped with a velvety, cheesy sauce? Yes, please! Be sure to check out the Meal prep it tip, as these taquitos come together in no time when you've planned ahead. They're great on their own, but for Sunday brunch, serve them with a Pretty Pitaya Bowl (page 43) and Savory Scrambled Tofu (page 49).

1. Fill a large pot with a few inches of water and bring to a boil. Place the potatoes in a steaming basket inside the pot, cover, and steam over medium heat for 10 minutes, or until almost tender. Add the kale. Steam for another 3 to 5 minutes, or until the kale is bright green and the potatoes are fully tender. Set aside.

2. Preheat the oven to 400°F.

3. Transfer the cooked potato cubes and kale to a bowl and mash with a fork or potato masher, until the potato is mostly smooth. Add the milk, garlic, salt, and pepper and stir well. Add the scallions and mix them in.

4. Warm the tortillas so they don't break: Rinse them lightly with water, then place on a nonstick (or silicone-lined) baking sheet. Bake for 2 to 3 minutes, or until soft and warm.

5. Transfer the tortillas to a flat surface, laying them out individually. Place an equal amount of the potato-kale filling in the center of each tortilla. Roll each tortilla up over the filling and into a small tube, then place seam-side down on the baking sheet. Cook for 15 minutes, or until the tortillas are golden brown and lightly crisp. Serve generously topped with the Low-Fat Cheese Dip and Classic Salsa (if using).

LEMON ROSEMARY POTATOES

SERVES 4

Prep Time: 10 minutes

Cook Time: 35 minutes

○ 30 MINUTES OR LESS
◑ GLUTEN-FREE
● LEFTOVER-FRIENDLY
○ NUT-FREE

2 tablespoons sunflower or olive oil, divided

1 cup sliced shallots

4 large unpeeled red or gold potatoes, cut into 1-inch pieces

2 tablespoons minced fresh rosemary

2 tablespoons freshly squeezed lemon juice

¾ teaspoon sea salt

¾ teaspoon freshly ground black pepper

It's potatoes like this that make a solid case for Sunday brunch, especially when served with some Blueberry Pancakes (page 56) and Strawberry Mylk (page 28). For an extra feast, serve up some Savory Scrambled Tofu (page 49) on the side as well, and be sure to have hot sauces around for your spicy friends, like me (I'm coming over if you serve these, just so you know).

1. In a large skillet or wok, heat 1 tablespoon of oil over medium-high heat. Cook the shallots for 3 to 5 minutes, stirring often, until the shallots soften and begin to brown.

2. Add the remaining 1 tablespoon of oil, the potatoes, and rosemary. Cook, stirring occasionally, for 20 to 25 minutes, or until the potatoes are golden brown and fork tender.

3. Add the lemon juice, salt, and pepper and cook for an additional minute. Serve hot or warm. Refrigerate leftovers in an airtight container for several days and reheat (and recrisp) in a toaster oven, oven, or air fryer.

Make it WFPB: Omit the oil and substitute water or vegetable broth. Also omit the salt.

Variation tip: For one of my favorite shortcuts, you can keep cooked, cooled baked potatoes on hand and use them instead of raw potatoes. Then, this dish will come together in about 10 minutes.

Per serving: Calories: 140; Fat: 5g; Carbohydrates: 19g; Fiber: 2g; Protein: 2g; Sodium: 1mg; Iron: 1mg

MEXICAN-INSPIRED POLENTA BOWL

SERVES 4

Prep Time: 10 minutes
Cook Time: 10 minutes

○ 30 MINUTES OR LESS
◉ GLUTEN-FREE
○ NUT-FREE

3 cups water

¾ cup dry polenta

3 tablespoons nutritional yeast

3 large garlic cloves, minced or pressed

¾ teaspoon sea salt

2 medium tomatoes, chopped

1 (15-ounce) can pinto beans, drained and rinsed, or 1½ cups cooked pinto beans (see page 17)

1 medium avocado, chopped

¼ cup diced scallions, both white and green parts

¼ cup chopped fresh cilantro

¼ cup raw or roasted pumpkin seeds

2 tablespoons minced jalapeño

1 fresh lime, quartered

There's something so breakfast-y about creamy polenta, and this version has some Mexican-inspired flair to boot. But it doesn't have to just live in your breakfast world. We often make this for dinner, too, served with some Tempeh Corn Chili (page 106) on the side. No matter what time of day you enjoy this, it's a dish that will stick with you for hours, as it has high levels of fiber and some healthy fats.

1. In a large pot, combine the water and polenta. Bring to a boil, stirring with a wire whisk. Reduce the heat to low and continue to whisk often for about 10 minutes, or until polenta is thick.

2. Whisk the nutritional yeast, garlic, and salt into the polenta mixture until smooth. Cook an additional minute.

3. Divide the polenta evenly into bowls and top each one with the tomatoes, pinto beans, avocado, scallions, cilantro, pumpkin seeds, and jalapeño. Serve with the lime wedges.

———————————

Substitution tip: This is also delicious with the Avotillo Sauce (page 201) instead of avocado. You can also use black-eyed peas instead of the pinto beans if you prefer. A final substitution option would be to crumble tortilla chips on top instead of pumpkin seeds for that added crunch.

Variation tip: If you prefer less heat, remove the seeds from the jalapeño before mincing.

Per serving: Calories: 331; Fat: 8g; Carbohydrates: 53g; Fiber: 10g; Protein: 14g; Sodium: 106mg; Iron: 3mg

CLASSIC FRENCH TOAST

SERVES 8

Prep Time: 10 minutes
Cook Time: 15 minutes

- GLUTEN-FREE
- LEFTOVER-FRIENDLY
- PLAN AHEAD

2 ripe peeled bananas, fresh or frozen

¾ cup unsweetened nondairy milk

¾ cup rolled oats

¼ cup unsalted raw whole cashews, soaked, drained, and rinsed (see page 11)

2 tablespoons nutritional yeast

1½ teaspoons ground cinnamon

1 teaspoon vanilla extract

⅛ teaspoon sea salt

8 slices bread of choice, cut diagonally into triangles

Variation tip: If you prefer a nut-free experience for any reason, you can simply omit the cashews and replace them with additional oats.

Per serving: Calories: 202; Fat: 5g; Carbohydrates: 32g; Fiber: 7g; Protein: 8g; Sodium: 178mg; Iron: 2mg

French toast is something that *everyone* will eat—people who think they hate vegan food, vegans who say they hate healthy food, picky kids, and everyone in between. I like to make a big batch of the batter, because it makes great leftovers. I store the batter in a container large enough to dip a slice of bread in, and pop it out during the week when French toast is required for happiness. You can top this with maple syrup, fresh fruit, applesauce, or anything else that sounds great.

1. In a blender, combine the bananas, milk, oats, cashews, nutritional yeast, cinnamon, vanilla, and salt. Blend until very smooth. Transfer the batter to a container that's big enough to dip a slice of bread in.

2. Heat a large skillet (or two, if you're making this whole batch now) over medium-high heat. If using a nonstick skillet, you won't need any oil. However, if you prefer to add some oil, heat 1 to 2 teaspoons per pan.

3. Dip the bread into the batter, thoroughly saturating it on all sides.

4. When the pan is hot, add the coated bread triangles, leaving a little room in between each piece. Cook for 2 to 3 minutes, or until golden brown on the bottom, and flip over. When golden brown on both sides, transfer to a plate.

5. Serve immediately with the topping(s) of your choice. Leftover batter will keep in an airtight container, refrigerated, for several days. However, the longer the batter is stored, the thicker it will become. If it becomes overly thick, simply thin it with a little nondairy milk.

BLUEBERRY PANCAKES

SERVES 4

Prep Time: 5 minutes
Cook Time: About 15 minutes

○ 30 MINUTES OR LESS
○ NUT-FREE

3 tablespoons water

2 tablespoons flaxseed meal

1 cup plain unsweetened nondairy milk

½ cup plain unsweetened nondairy yogurt

1 teaspoon vanilla extract

1 cup whole-wheat pastry flour

1 teaspoon baking powder

½ teaspoon baking soda

⅛ teaspoon sea salt

½ cup blueberries

Variation tip: You can easily swap out the blueberries for another type of berry—my daughter's favorite is sliced strawberries. We also like making these with diced apples and adding a little cinnamon. Yum!

Per serving: Calories: 165; Fat: 5g; Carbohydrates: 28g; Fiber: 6g; Protein: 5g; Sodium: 312mg; Iron: 1mg

Who wants pancakes? Everyone, basically. But here's what's really cool—these delicious pancakes are free from refined flours and sugars. Plus, they have the benefits of flax and blueberries, which will give your body a happy little antioxidant and fiber boost.

1. Mix the water and flaxseed meal in a medium bowl. Set aside for 5 minutes or until thick and gooey.

2. Once the mixture has thickened, stir in the milk, yogurt, and vanilla until well combined.

3. Add the flour, baking powder, baking soda, and salt and stir just until combined (don't overmix). Gently stir in the blueberries.

4. Heat a large skillet over medium-high heat. If using a nonstick skillet, you won't need any oil. However, if you prefer to add some oil (coconut or sunflower work well), heat 1 to 2 teaspoons.

5. Once it's hot, pour 3 tablespoons of batter per pancake into the pan. Don't make the pancakes too big or they'll be hard to flip. Repeat, adding more batter to create additional pancakes, allowing 2 inches of space between each.

6. Flip each pancake after 2 minutes, or as soon as the undersides are brown (they'll be crisp around the edges and bubbly on top). When both sides are golden brown, transfer to a plate. Continue this process until all of the batter has been used up. Serve immediately with maple syrup, jam, applesauce, or anything else that makes you smile.

BLUEBERRY-BANANA BUCKWHEAT CRUNCH PANCAKES

SERVES 4

Prep Time: 5 minutes
Cook Time: 20 minutes

- ● GLUTEN-FREE
- ○ NUT-FREE
- ● PLAN AHEAD

1 large very ripe banana

1¼ cups unsweetened nondairy milk

½ cup brown rice flour or whole-wheat pastry flour

¼ cup buckwheat flour or additional brown rice flour or whole-wheat pastry flour

¼ cup Buckwheat Crisps (page 199)

½ teaspoon baking powder

¼ teaspoon sea salt

½ cup blueberries, fresh or frozen

I used to avoid pancakes because I thought of them as unhealthy, refined-carb energy drainers. However, these plant-powered pancakes are just the opposite. They're overflowing with nutrient-dense ingredients and contain zero added sugars, fats, or refined flours. If you want super hearty pancakes, you can even use all buckwheat flour here, although the brown rice or whole-wheat pastry flour helps make them lighter.

1. In a large bowl, using a fork, mash the banana well. Add the milk and stir well to combine. Add the flours, Buckwheat Crisps, baking powder, and salt. Stir just until thoroughly combined. Gently stir in the blueberries.

2. Heat a large skillet over medium-high heat. If using a nonstick skillet, you won't need any oil. However, if you prefer to add some oil, heat 1 to 2 teaspoons.

3. Once the pan is hot, pour in 3 tablespoons of batter per pancake. Don't make your pancakes too big or they'll be hard to flip. Repeat, adding more batter to create additional pancakes, allowing 2 inches of space between each.

4. Cook for 1 to 2 minutes, or until the undersides are browned, then flip each pancake. Cook for another 1 to 2 minutes. Once both sides are golden brown, transfer to a plate and serve.

Variation tip: For an extra treat, serve these with blueberry maple syrup: Simply cook the amount of maple syrup you'd like to top your pancakes along with a handful or two of blueberries in a small pot over low heat, whisking well until heated through. The blueberries should pop and turn the syrup purple. You can even mash them in to make the syrup more incorporated.

Per serving: Calories: 158; Fat: 2g; Carbohydrates: 34g; Fiber: 5g; Protein: 4g; Sodium: 107mg; Iron: 1mg

Maple Shishitos, page 67

CHAPTER FIVE

SNACKS AND SIDES

POPPED AMARANTH

SERVES 2 TO 3

Prep Time: Less than 1 minute

Cook Time: 10 to 15 minutes

○ 30 MINUTES OR LESS
◉ GLUTEN-FREE
○ NUT-FREE

¼ cup whole amaranth

2 teaspoons refined coconut, sunflower, or avocado oil

Sea salt

Fun fact: Unlike with popcorn, I love to let the natural, wild, wonderful flavor of the amaranth come through, hence the simple seasoning here.

Per serving: Calories: 83; Fat: 4g; Carbohydrates: 10g; Fiber: 2g; Protein: 2g; Sodium: 0mg; Iron: 1mg

Imagine the world's tiniest, cutest popcorn, and you'll have popped amaranth. This unusual snack is available in any health food store and surprisingly nutrient-dense. If the directions below seem long, it's because popped amaranth can burn easily, and I want you to have all of the details you need to succeed.

1. Get the materials ready: You'll need a medium or large pot with a tight-fitting, see-through lid. Choose something with a slippery surface such as steel, copper, or nonstick (*not* cast iron, for example) so that the amaranth can easily slide around. Have a medium-sized bowl handy as well.

2. Next, get your pan to *just* the right temperature. Place it over medium-high heat and add about 3 amaranth grains to the pot. Cover with the lid and watch. Once the amaranth grains turn dark brown, discard and add just enough new amaranth to barely cover the bottom of the pot in a single layer. All of the amaranth needs to be touching the hot surface. I use about 1 teaspoon of amaranth per batch for a medium-sized pot.

3. As soon as those amaranth grains go in, immediately begin shaking the pot. The grains will begin to pop—don't stop shaking until the popping slows down, then immediately empty into the bowl. If you wait too long, the amaranth will burn.

4. Continue popping the amaranth in batches until you're all out of amaranth, or you've gotten too hungry to go on.

5. To season: If you're using coconut oil, melt it in the pan and drizzle it over the amaranth. Other types of oil can be poured straight onto the amaranth. Season with salt and stir well. Enjoy immediately.

QUICKLES

SERVES 4

Prep Time: 2 to 3 minutes

○ 30 MINUTES OR LESS
◐ GLUTEN-FREE
● LEFTOVER-FRIENDLY
○ NUT-FREE

2 medium cucumbers or 1 large English cucumber (about 1 pound)

1½ tablespoons freshly squeezed lime juice

¼ teaspoon sea salt

As the name would imply, these are indeed quick! I almost feel guilty giving you a recipe for these, but here's why I can still sleep at night: In all my years of cooking, being vegan, and striving to eat lots of vegetables, I'd never thought of doing these quick "pickles" until recently, and now I make them almost every week. It's a good way to give an extra flavor punch to regular cucumbers, and a health-boosting alternative to packaged snacks when you just want to crunch on something.

1. Wash the cucumber (no need to peel) and cut it into spears, about 2 inches long and ½-inch wide.

2. Place in a bowl and toss with the lime juice and salt. Eat immediately or refrigerate in an airtight container for up to 4 days.

Variation tip: For Garlic-Dill Quickles, add the following to the basic recipe: 1 teaspoon dried dill, ½ teaspoon garlic granules or powder, and ¼ teaspoon freshly ground black pepper. Toss and serve or refrigerate for later.

Per serving: Calories: 18; Fat: 0g; Carbohydrates: 4g; Fiber: 1g; Protein: 3g; Sodium: 12mg; Iron: 0mg

CINNAMON ROLL ENERGY BITES

MAKES ABOUT 18 BITES

Prep Time: 10 minutes

○ 30 MINUTES OR LESS
◐ GLUTEN-FREE
● LEFTOVER-FRIENDLY

1 cup walnuts

1 packed cup raisins

1 tablespoon ground cinnamon

¼ teaspoon sea salt

¼ teaspoon ground nutmeg

I have so much love for (and a bordering obsession with) energy cookies like this. They're perfect for traveling or just running errands, as they're chock-full of nutrient-dense ingredients to keep you going for hours. These obviously aren't cinnamon rolls in the traditional sense, but the flavor will remind you of one. They're not just delicious, but also brain-boosting, and one of those snacks you'll always want to keep on hand.

1. In a food processor, combine the walnuts, raisins, cinnamon, salt, and nutmeg. Blend until the mixture balls up and sticks together. You're aiming to thoroughly combine all of the ingredients, yet retain a little texture.

2. With your hands, roll the mixture into 1-inch balls. Refrigerate in an airtight container for up to 2 months.

First-timer tip: People often ask me if these energy bites can be made in a blender rather than a food processor. And unfortunately, my answer is always, "Not any blender I've ever used." The wide base of a food processor is necessary for this type of dense mixture.

Per serving (1 bite): Calories: 71; Fat: 5g; Carbohydrates: 8g; Fiber: 1g; Protein: 1g; Sodium: 0mg; Iron: 0mg

LEMONY POTATO VEGGIE BAKE

SERVES 6

Prep Time: 10 minutes
Cook Time: About 1 hour

○ GLUTEN-FREE
● LEFTOVER-FRIENDLY
○ NUT-FREE

3½ cups finely diced potatoes (any variety, but red or gold are ideal)

1 (15-ounce) can chickpeas, drained and rinsed, or 1½ cups cooked chickpeas (see page 17)

1 medium red bell pepper, chopped

½ large white or yellow onion, chopped

1 cup broccoli florets

¼ cup freshly squeezed lemon juice

1 tablespoon olive oil

1 teaspoon sea salt

½ teaspoon freshly ground black pepper

This simple side dish has become a staple at our house because it's delicious, it makes great leftovers, and it's pretty to look at. Plus, you can vary the vegetables you use depending on what's in season and in your refrigerator. We also like to use sweet potatoes, cauliflower, and zucchini. One of my favorite things about this bake is the addition of the chickpeas, because they become enticingly chewy (and sometimes crisp) upon roasting.

1. Preheat the oven to 400°F.

2. In a large bowl, combine the potatoes, chickpeas, bell pepper, onion, broccoli, lemon juice, oil, salt, and pepper and toss well to combine.

3. Transfer to two large nonstick baking sheets and spread into single layers. Bake for 30 minutes. Toss and bake for another 20 to 30 minutes, or until the vegetables are browned and tender. Be sure to check often after the first 30 to 40 minutes of baking, as the time will vary depending on your oven, size of your vegetable pieces, and the types of baking sheets you use.

4. Remove and enjoy. Refrigerate leftovers in an airtight container for up to a week.

Make it WFPB: Bake on silicone or nonstick sheets to avoid using oil. Omit the salt.

Variation tip: You can also add fresh herbs to this bake for added flavor. Rosemary, basil, and oregano are all great choices. If using basil, sprinkle it fresh over the cooked veggies after you take them out of the oven.

Per serving: Calories: 119; Fat: 2g; Carbohydrates: 16g; Fiber: 3g; Protein: 2g; Sodium: 51mg; Iron: 1mg

CLASSIC GUACAMOLE

SERVES 4

Prep Time: 10 minutes

○ 30 MINUTES OR LESS
◉ GLUTEN-FREE
○ NUT-FREE

2 medium ripe avocados, halved and pitted

2 tablespoons freshly squeezed lime juice

2 tablespoons minced fresh cilantro

2 large garlic cloves, minced or pressed

½ teaspoon sea salt

I've found that the perfect guacamole is actually pretty simple—plenty of lime and garlic, with just the right amount of salt to ensure that the flavor pops. You can enjoy this as a dip with tortilla chips, raw vegetables, or crackers—or as a topping for tacos, tostadas, burritos, or bowls. Basically, anywhere you want some extra avocado love in your food.

In a bowl, using a fork, mash the avocados. Stir in the lime juice, cilantro, garlic, and salt. Serve immediately. Refrigerate leftovers in an airtight container and use within a day or so for optimal freshness.

Variation tip: My partner, John, likes to take this guacamole a step further and make it an absolute party. Here's what he adds to the basic guacamole recipe: 1 minced jalapeño, ¼ cup pomegranate seeds, 2 tablespoons minced red onion or scallions, and 1 tablespoon diced shallot. He usually minces up ½ teaspoon habanero to add to it, too, but if you're not into heat, proceed with caution, as habaneros are extremely hot. And be sure to wear gloves if you work with hot peppers, so you don't accidentally rub your eyes with spicy fingers! I've been there, and it's not pretty.

Per serving: Calories: 113; Fat: 10g; Carbohydrates: 7g; Fiber: 5g; Protein: 2g; Sodium: 5mg; Iron: 0mg

EDAMAME MISO HUMMUS

SERVES 6 TO 8

Prep Time: 10 minutes

○ 30 MINUTES OR LESS
◐ GLUTEN-FREE
● LEFTOVER-FRIENDLY
○ NUT-FREE

1¼ cups shelled edamame, thawed if frozen

½ cup tahini

½ cup baby spinach

5 tablespoons freshly squeezed lime juice

2 tablespoons water

1½ tablespoons mellow white miso

3 large garlic cloves, peeled

½ teaspoon sea salt

This is an incredibly flavorful, nutrient-dense twist on regular hummus. Miso is detoxifying and immune-boosting, and the tahini and lime join in to create the perfect flavor balance. You can serve this life-changing dip with crackers, raw veggies, baked tortilla crisps, or even as a sandwich spread.

In a blender, combine the edamame, tahini, spinach, lime juice, water, miso, garlic, and salt. Blend until completely smooth. Serve cold or at room temperature. Refrigerate in an airtight container for up to a week.

———————————

Variation tip: Want something fun for the holidays? Make up a batch of this green hummus as directed above. Then, make up a "red" batch by substituting chickpeas for the edamame and roasted red pepper for the spinach. Serve them side by side in a large dish, sprinkled lightly with finely chopped parsley or cilantro. Alternatively, you can simply top the original recipe with some pomegranate seeds for that red and green holiday vibe.

Per serving: Calories: 131; Fat: 10g; Carbohydrates: 6g; Fiber: 3g; Protein: 6g; Sodium: 144mg; Iron: 2mg

MAPLE SHISHITOS

SERVES 4

Prep Time: 1 minute

Cook Time: 10 minutes or less

- ○ 30 MINUTES OR LESS
- ● GLUTEN-FREE
- ○ NUT-FREE

Nonstick cooking spray (coconut oil)

1 pound shishito peppers, rinsed (no need to remove stems)

2 tablespoons maple syrup

4 teaspoons freshly squeezed lemon juice

¾ teaspoon sea salt

Craving a satisfying snack, but trying to avoid greasy foods? Try a big bowl of shishitos instead. They taste like a very mild, full-flavored pepper (unless you get a rare hot one). Whenever I'm at a farmers' market, the first thing I do is scope out local shishito peppers (and happy-scream if I find some). They also tend to turn up in health food stores and grocery chains such as Sprouts and Trader Joe's.

1. Preheat the oven to broil. Spray a baking sheet with cooking spray.

2. Place the peppers in a single layer on the baking sheet and spray the tops with oil. Roast until the shishitos are browned with charred patches on them. This should take less than 10 minutes, so check on them every 2 minutes or so to prevent burning.

3. Remove from the oven. If they look dry, spritz with the oil again.

4. In a large bowl, toss the peppers with the maple syrup, lemon juice, and salt. Serve immediately.

_____

First-timer tip: If you've never had shishitos before, you're in for a treat. Just grab them by the stem and eat the rest of the pepper. Discard the stem and repeat, repeat, repeat!

Per serving: Calories: 52; Fat: 0g; Carbohydrates: 12g; Fiber: 1g; Protein: 3g; Sodium: 15mg; Iron: 0mg

GARLIC MASHED POTATOES

SERVES 4

Prep Time: 5 minutes

Cook Time: 25 minutes

○ GLUTEN-FREE
○ PLAN AHEAD

2 pounds russet or gold potatoes, peeled and chopped (6 cups)

1 cup water

½ cup raw unsalted whole cashews, soaked, drained, and rinsed (see page 11)

4 large garlic cloves, pressed or minced

1 teaspoon sea salt

½ teaspoon freshly ground black pepper

I used to think of mashed potatoes as a special treat, probably because they're usually made with rich, processed ingredients. Before creating this dish, I made mashed potatoes maybe twice a year, tops. But with this simple, delicious recipe—made mostly from plant-strong whole foods—they're healthy enough to eat all the time. How awesome is that? Try them plain or topped with Eat-It-Every-Day Gravy (page 211).

1. Fill a large pot with a few inches of water and bring to a boil. Place the potatoes in a steaming basket inside the pot. Cover and steam over medium heat for 25 minutes, or until fork tender.

2. Meanwhile, in a blender, combine the water and cashews. Blend until very smooth. Set aside.

3. Drain the potatoes and transfer to a large bowl. Mash well with a potato masher or fork.

4. Add the cashew cream, garlic, salt, and pepper and whip with electric beaters, starting on low, then increasing to high, until very smooth and fluffy. Serve hot or warm, plain or with Eat-It-Every-Day Gravy.

Variation tip: If you like, fold in 2 tablespoons or more minced chives before whipping. You can also squeeze a little lemon juice on top. For another variation, top these with caramelized shallots or onions, or even serve drizzled with Cheesy Sauce (page 210).

Make it WFPB: Omit the salt, or use a little mellow white miso instead (begin with 1 tablespoon and add more if needed).

Per serving: Calories: 126; Fat: 3g; Carbohydrates: 23g; Fiber: 2g; Protein: 4g; Sodium: 1mg; Iron: 1mg

GINGER-GLAZED BOK CHOY

SERVES 3

Prep Time: 5 minutes

Cook Time: 2 minutes

○ 30 MINUTES OR LESS

● GLUTEN-FREE

○ NUT-FREE

1 pound bok choy, chopped (about 16 cups)

¼ cup water

3 tablespoons minced fresh ginger

3 tablespoons tamari, shoyu, or soy sauce

1 tablespoon neutral-flavored oil (sunflower, sesame, or avocado)

2 tablespoons arrowroot powder

This recipe is on regular rotation at our house, because John and I love ginger too much, and also because this dish only takes seven minutes, start to finish. You may need to adjust your water and arrowroot amounts, depending on the density of your bok choy, so if it's a little too dry, add more water. And if it's not thick enough, sprinkle in more arrowroot. You're going for a lightly glazed result here. Enjoy, my fellow ginger lovers.

1. In a large wok or skillet, combine the bok choy, water, ginger, tamari, and oil over medium-high heat.

2. Stir well, then sprinkle the arrowroot evenly over the top. Stir it in immediately. Cook for about 2 minutes, stirring constantly, until the bok choy is wilted and crisp-tender. Serve immediately.

Variation tip: This also works well with greens such as kale or collards. Simply substitute them for the bok choy. For another twist on this dish, use chopped garlic in place of the ginger (however, if you do that, be sure to sauté it in the oil for a minute before adding the other ingredients for a mellow, rich garlic flavor).

Make it WFPB: Substitute additional water for the oil.

Per serving: Calories: 74; Fat: 5g; Carbohydrates: 6g; Fiber: 0g; Protein: 2g; Sodium: 1010mg; Iron: 0mg

MISO-TAHINI BRUSSELS SPROUTS

SERVES 4

Prep Time: 10 minutes
Cook Time: 15 minutes

- ○ 30 MINUTES OR LESS
- ● GLUTEN-FREE
- ○ NUT-FREE
- ○ WFPB

4 cups Brussels sprouts, trimmed and halved

2 tablespoons raw tahini

2 tablespoons mellow white miso

2 teaspoons freshly squeezed lime juice

2 teaspoons water

1 teaspoon black sesame seeds

I have no idea why the combination of tahini and miso is so enticing, but I won't question it, especially because they're both such nutritional powerhouses. Tahini is a great source of iron and calcium, and miso is detoxifying and immune-boosting. These Brussels sprouts are best served immediately and make for a simple, tasty meal alongside the Simple Staple Rice (page 134) and some soup, such as the Red Lentil Dal (page 108).

1. Preheat the oven to 400°F.

2. On a large nonstick baking sheet, place the Brussels sprouts and bake for 15 minutes, or until tender and well browned.

3. While the Brussels sprouts are cooking, in a large bowl, combine the tahini, miso, lime juice, and water. Whisk well until smooth.

4. Place the Brussels sprouts in the bowl and toss well with the sauce. Serve sprinkled with the sesame seeds.

Ingredient tip: Tahini can vary greatly in thickness, depending on which brand you buy. For this recipe, I used Whole Foods organic tahini, which is relatively thin. If your tahini is extremely thick, simply add a little more water to the sauce so that you're able to stir it.

Variation tip: If you prefer, steam the Brussels sprouts instead of roasting them in the oven. They'll take about 10 minutes in a covered pot to become just tender and bright green.

Per serving: Calories: 120; Fat: 6g; Carbohydrates: 13g; Fiber: 5g; Protein: 6g; Sodium: 353mg; Iron: 2mg

LUSCIOUS EGGPLANT

SERVES 4

Prep Time: 5 minutes
Cook Time: 16 minutes

○ 30 MINUTES OR LESS
◉ GLUTEN-FREE
○ NUT-FREE

1 pound eggplant, preferably Japanese, cubed (6 cups)

2½ cups water

20 small fresh curry leaves (optional)

4 teaspoons maple syrup

1 tablespoon tamari, shoyu, or soy sauce

3 large garlic cloves, minced or pressed

2 teaspoons toasted sesame oil

¼ to ½ teaspoon red pepper flakes

This dish, although very healthy, is absolutely luscious. It serves four, but if you're eggplant-obsessed like me, you may want to send your family away so you can hoard this all to yourself. I get the curry leaves at a local Asian market, but they can be hard to locate if you don't have access to international supermarkets. If you can't find them, don't worry—this will still be satisfying and delicious without. Enjoy this dish by itself or alongside Simple Staple Rice (page 134).

1. In a large skillet or wok, combine the eggplant, water, and curry leaves (if using) over medium-high heat. Cook for 10 to 12 minutes, stirring occasionally, until the eggplant is tender. If the pan becomes dry before the eggplant is tender, add more water.

2. Add the maple syrup, tamari, garlic, oil, and red pepper flakes. Stir-fry for another 3 to 4 minutes, or until the eggplant is very tender and has a browned, glazed appearance. Serve immediately.

Make it WFPB: Use extra water instead of the sesame oil, and garnish with a generous sprinkle of toasted sesame seeds.

Per serving: Calories: 44; Fat: 2g; Carbohydrates: 6g; Fiber: 0g; Protein: 1g; Sodium: 253mg; Iron: 0mg

PIZZA HUMMUS

MAKES ABOUT 2 CUPS

Prep Time: 10 minutes

- ○ 30 MINUTES OR LESS
- ◑ GLUTEN-FREE
- ● LEFTOVER-FRIENDLY
- ○ NUT-FREE

1 (15-ounce) can chickpeas, rinsed and drained, or 1½ cups cooked chickpeas (see page 17)

1 cup tomato sauce

¼ cup nutritional yeast

¼ cup water

3 tablespoons extra-virgin olive oil

3 large garlic cloves, peeled

1 tablespoon dried oregano

1 tablespoon dried rosemary

1 tablespoon dried basil

1 tablespoon balsamic vinegar

1 teaspoon sea salt

3 tablespoons thinly sliced fresh basil, for garnish (optional)

¼ cup pitted chopped kalamata olives, for garnish (optional)

With the plethora of hummus varieties on the market today, you may be wondering why you should make your own at home. Here's my reply—homemade anything is always less processed, and homemade hummus is almost always more delicious and fresh-tasting than store-bought. Serve this pizza-flavored hummus with baked pita chips, crackers, or even over baked potatoes or pasta.

1. In a blender, combine the chickpeas, tomato sauce, nutritional yeast, water, oil, garlic, oregano, rosemary, basil, vinegar, and salt. Blend until completely smooth.

2. Transfer to a bowl and serve, garnished with basil and olives (if using), or refrigerate in an airtight container for up to a week.

Make it WFPB: Substitute additional water for the olive oil and omit the salt.

Fun fact: One of my recipe testers loved this dip and suggested it as a protein-rich alternative to pizza sauce! I haven't tried that yet, but I loved the idea so much I had to share it with you.

Per recipe: Calories: 223; Fat: 8g; Carbohydrates: 19g; Fiber: 5g; Protein: 6g; Sodium: 353mg; Iron: 3mg

BUTTER BEAN SMASH

SERVES 4

Prep Time: 5 minutes

Cook Time: 2 to 3 minutes

○ 30 MINUTES OR LESS
◐ GLUTEN-FREE
● LEFTOVER-FRIENDLY
○ NUT-FREE

2 (15-ounce) cans butter beans, rinsed and drained, or 3 cups cooked butter beans (see page 17)

2 tablespoons plain unsweetened nondairy milk

4 teaspoons sunflower or olive oil

4 teaspoons red wine vinegar

2 to 3 large garlic cloves, minced or pressed

¾ teaspoon sea salt

¼ teaspoon freshly ground black pepper

2 tablespoons finely chopped fresh chives (optional)

Butter beans are aptly named—they're so creamy and soft. But if you've never tried them before, you're in good company. Even after almost three decades of being vegan (and even longer of being a bean-lover), I didn't try them until recently. I use Eden brand because they cook their beans thoroughly and use kombu in the process (which helps make beans more digestible and adds nutrients). Butter beans are a yummy, fiber-rich side for weeknights or holidays and are especially delicious with a little Eat-It-Every-Day Gravy (page 211) poured on top.

1. In a medium pot, combine the beans, milk, oil, vinegar, garlic, salt, and pepper. Stir very well, until as "smashed" as possible. If you desire a fluffier, smoother result, whip with electric beaters, starting on low, then increasing to high, until fluffy.

2. Heat over low heat for 2 to 3 minutes until warmed through, stirring often. Serve topped with the chives (if using). Refrigerate leftovers in an airtight container for up to 5 days.

Make it WFPB: Replace the oil with more of the nondairy milk.

Per serving: Calories: 210; Fat: 5g; Carbohydrates: 27g; Fiber: 8g; Protein: 10g; Sodium: 660mg; Iron: 3mg

CHILI-GINGER CABBAGE

SERVES 4 TO 6

Prep Time: 10 minutes
Cook Time: 5 minutes

○ 30 MINUTES OR LESS
◑ GLUTEN-FREE
● LEFTOVER-FRIENDLY
○ NUT-FREE

6 cups finely chopped green cabbage

¼ cup water

¼ cup plus 2 tablespoons freshly squeezed lime juice

¼ cup fresh ginger, finely chopped or julienned

3 tablespoons agave nectar

1 teaspoon red pepper flakes

¾ teaspoon sea salt

I first had this dish at a place called Panda Forest in my college town of Kalamazoo, Michigan, and I quickly became obsessed. Although simple, it was addictive, and I found myself trying (and failing) to re-create it at home. Finally, the happy day came when I was successful, and ever since it has been one of my all-time favorite side dishes. I love the tang of the lime paired with the heat of the ginger and chili. This is delicious served with Immune-Boosting Lime-Ginger-Miso Noodles (page 146), or even just alongside brown rice for a simple, clean meal on the go.

1. In a large skillet or wok, sauté the cabbage in the water over medium-high heat, stirring often, for 5 minutes, or just until it becomes slightly wilted. Transfer to a large bowl.

2. Add the lime juice, ginger, agave, red pepper flakes, and salt to the bowl and stir well.

3. Place in an airtight container and refrigerate for an hour or more. Stir well and serve cold or at room temperature. Refrigerate leftovers in an airtight container for up to a week.

_____

Substitution tip: If you prefer an alternative to agave, use coconut sugar instead.

Per serving: Calories: 63; Fat: 1g; Carbohydrates: 15g; Fiber: 0g; Protein: 2g; Sodium: 16mg; Iron: 0mg

YELLOW SPLIT PEA ROLLS WITH BERBERE SAUCE

MAKES 16 ROLLS

Prep Time: 10 minutes

Cook Time: 20 minutes

- ◑ GLUTEN-FREE
- ● LEFTOVER-FRIENDLY
- ○ NUT-FREE
- ◑ PLAN AHEAD

FOR THE ROLLS

16 spring roll rice paper wraps (I prefer brown rice paper)

Ethiopian-Spiced Yellow Split Peas (page 113)

Nonstick cooking spray (coconut or sunflower oil)

FOR THE BERBERE SAUCE

2 tablespoons neutral-flavored oil

2½ cups chopped white or yellow onions

¼ cup plus 2 tablespoons water

2 tablespoons berbere

1 teaspoon sea salt

Make it WFPB: Omit the oil in the sauce and use extra water instead. You can also omit the oil spray on top of the rolls before baking. Omit the salt.

Per serving (2 rolls): Calories: 177; Fat: 5g; Carbohydrates: 29g; Fiber: 5g; Protein: 3g; Sodium: 663mg; Iron: 0mg

If you're unfamiliar, berbere is a traditional (and divine!) Ethiopian spice blend. Serve these rolls as a snack on their own, or alongside some Red Lentil Dal (page 108) or Creamy Dreamy Lentils (page 109) for a meal.

TO MAKE THE ROLLS

1. Preheat the oven to 400°F.

2. Gently take a rice paper wrap and run it under warm water until thoroughly moistened on both sides. Lay flat on a nonporous surface and fill with about ¼ cup of the Ethiopian-Spiced Yellow Split Peas.

3. Wrap the bottom up and over the filling, then fold in the sides. Finish by rolling all the way up from the bottom, as if you were rolling a burrito. Repeat this process to make as many rolls as you plan to eat at this moment. The leftover split peas will keep in the refrigerator for up to a week, or can be frozen for months.

4. Place the rolls on a lightly oiled or nonstick baking sheet. Lightly spray the top of the rolls with cooking spray and bake for 15 to 20 minutes, or until just crisp.

5. Allow the rolls to cool for a few minutes, then serve with the berbere sauce for dipping. Both will keep for 2 weeks in the refrigerator or months in the freezer.

TO MAKE THE BERBERE SAUCE

1. While the rolls are cooking, in a large pan, heat the oil over medium heat and caramelize the onions in the oil for 10 to 20 minutes, stirring often, until browned and soft. Remove from the heat and transfer to a blender.

2. Add the water, berbere, and salt and blend until very smooth.

FRESH SPRING ROLLS WITH PEANUT SAUCE

MAKES 8 SPRING ROLLS

Prep Time: 25 minutes

- ● GLUTEN-FREE
- ● PLAN AHEAD
- ○ WFPB

Everything Tofu (page 212)

1 large carrot, grated or julienned

½ cup grated or finely chopped
purple cabbage

¼ cucumber, thinly sliced into 2-inch strips

½ cup chopped fresh cilantro

½ cup chopped fresh basil

2 tablespoons minced fresh mint

1 to 2 scallions, both white and green
parts, minced

8 spring roll rice paper wraps (preferably
made from brown rice)

1 cup Peanut Sauce, Two Ways (page 207)
(either version)

First-timer tip: Refrigerate leftovers
in an airtight container for up to a day,
especially if covered with a wet paper
towel. However, they are much better fresh,
so I recommend only making as many as
you plan to eat on the spot. Also, be sure
not to overfill the wraps or they'll break.
However, if the worst happens and they
break or tear open, good news! You can
double-wrap them, or patch with another
piece of softened spring roll wrapper.

Per serving (2 rolls): Calories: 402; Fat: 15g;
Carbohydrates: 43g; Fiber: 5g; Protein:
28g; Sodium: 697mg; Iron: 4mg

I've gotten in trouble for saying "I could eat these every day" about too many types of food, but I really *do* eat these spring rolls almost every day. In fact, I had some before writing this recipe! They're one of those foods I never tire of, even after decades of obsession. Although you can vary the ingredients as you like (such as adding in some bean thread or brown rice vermicelli noodles), it's important to keep some fresh herbs for maximum flavor. I've used the holy trinity of Thai herbs here—cilantro, mint, and basil. If you like things spicy, add a splash of sriracha sauce.

1. On a clean workspace, in individual bowls, arrange all of the fillings (the Everything Tofu, carrot, cabbage, cucumber, cilantro, basil, mint, and scallions) so they're accessible.

2. Gently take a rice paper wrap and run it under warm water until thoroughly moistened on both sides. Lay flat on a nonporous surface. Place a little of each filling item onto the wrapper in a horizontal line toward the bottom. Once the rice paper is fully softened, roll the bottom of the wrapper up and over the fillings. Next, fold the left and right sides over the filling, maintaining parallel lines, then roll all the way up from the bottom. The rice paper will self-seal. Set aside and repeat this process until all of the fillings are used.

3. Serve with the Peanut Sauce for dipping.

Ingredient tip: Spring roll wraps are available in any Asian market, most supermarkets, and health food stores. I use Star Anise Foods brand brown rice wrappers.

Rainbow Quinoa Salad,
page 86

CHAPTER SIX

SALADS

WATERMELON SUMMER SALAD

SERVES 4

Prep Time: 5 to 10 minutes

○ 30 MINUTES OR LESS
◐ GLUTEN-FREE
● LEFTOVER-FRIENDLY
○ NUT-FREE
○ WFPB

8 cups chopped watermelon

4 cups sliced strawberries

3 tablespoons freshly squeezed lime juice

2 teaspoons minced fresh mint or basil (optional)

This salad is the epitome of summer. My friend Christina made it for me years ago, and I realized for the first time that watermelon should never be allowed to leave the house without fresh lime juice by its side. They pair so well it's almost criminal. In fact, in my house, no one eats watermelon anymore without a little lime juice squeezed on top. You'll find that the amount of lime juice needed will vary depending on the sweetness of your watermelon, so adjust accordingly. I sometimes prefer this without the fresh herbs if I'm really going for simplicity.

In a bowl, toss the watermelon, strawberries, lime juice, and mint (if using) until well combined and serve. Refrigerate leftovers in an airtight container for 2 to 3 days.

———————

Substitution tip: You can use blueberries instead of the strawberries if you prefer—or go half and half.

Variation tip: Add pomegranate seeds instead of (or in addition to) the mint or basil. You can also use dried or fresh cherries in place of some (or all) of the strawberries. For another twist, omit the lime juice and splash the salad with a little balsamic vinegar or balsamic reduction (in which case, the fresh basil pairs perfectly).

Per serving: Calories: 144; Fat: 0g; Carbohydrates: 36g; Fiber: 3g; Protein: 3g; Sodium: 3mg; Iron: 1mg

5-INGREDIENT GO-TO SALAD

SERVES 1

Prep Time: 2 to 5 minutes

- ○ 30 MINUTES OR LESS
- ● GLUTEN-FREE
- ○ NUT-FREE
- ○ WFPB

1 tablespoon raw tahini

2 teaspoons coconut aminos

½ tablespoon freshly squeezed lime juice

3 cups lettuce of choice (I use romaine or baby greens)

1 small carrot, grated or ½ cup diced cucumber

This salad is extremely quick and easy to make (I love any dish that can be made in one bowl, start to finish), and overflowing with nutrients. This recipe makes a heaping individual serving (for someone like me who loves a *big* salad), but of course you can double or triple it if you're feeding a crowd. To make this a main dish, add some Everything Tofu (page 212).

1. In a large bowl, combine the tahini, coconut aminos, and lime juice. Whisk until smooth. If your tahini is very thick, you may need to add a little water as you go.

2. Add the lettuce and carrot and stir with a rubber spatula. Serve immediately.

Ingredient tip: Coconut aminos are a mellow, slightly sweet alternative to soy sauce or tamari that I absolutely love. Find it at any health food store and many supermarkets (we buy ours at Costco).

Per serving: Calories: 156; Fat: 10g; Carbohydrates: 16g; Fiber: 7g; Protein: 6g; Sodium: 279mg; Iron: 3mg

ARUGULA SALAD WITH MISO-GOJI DRESSING

SERVES 6

Prep Time: 10 minutes

- ◑ GLUTEN-FREE
- ● LEFTOVER-FRIENDLY
- ○ PLAN AHEAD
- ○ WFPB

FOR THE MISO-GOJI DRESSING

½ cup raw unsalted whole cashews, soaked, drained, and rinsed (see page 11)

¼ cup dried goji berries, soaked for 1 to 2 hours and drained

½ cup chopped white or yellow onion

½ cup water

¼ cup nutritional yeast

¼ cup red miso

¼ cup balsamic vinegar

FOR THE SALAD

6 cups baby arugula

6 cups baby greens

1 small cucumber, diced

¼ cup raisins

I love this salad to the point of obsession. It's easy to make, ridiculously high in nutrients (hello, goji, miso, and nutritional yeast), and of course, absolutely delicious. As with any recipe containing cashews, if you have a high-speed blender (such as Vitamix or Blendtec), you can skip soaking the cashews and goji berries.

TO MAKE THE MISO-GOJI DRESSING

In a blender, combine the soaked cashews and goji berries, along with the onion, water, nutritional yeast, miso, and vinegar. Blend until completely emulsified and smooth.

TO MAKE THE SALAD

In a large bowl, toss the arugula, baby greens, cucumber, and raisins or divide between individual bowls and drizzle with the desired amount of dressing. Serve immediately.

Batch cooking tip: If you love this dressing even half as much as I do, feel free to double or triple the dressing recipe and keep it on hand. It also livens up rice or roasted vegetables. Store in the refrigerator in an airtight container for several weeks.

Ingredient tip: Feel free to soak the cashews and goji berries in the same bowl. No need to separate them.

Per serving: Calories: 180; Fat: 5g; Carbohydrates: 31g; Fiber: 3g; Protein: 8g; Sodium: 476mg; Iron: 2mg

SPINACH SALAD WITH SESAME-GINGER-ORANGE DRESSING

SERVES 4

Prep Time: 10 minutes

- ○ 30 MINUTES OR LESS
- ● GLUTEN-FREE
- ○ NUT-FREE
- ○ WFPB

FOR THE DRESSING

¼ cup tahini

¼ cup orange juice

2 tablespoons grated fresh ginger

2 tablespoons coconut sugar

1 tablespoon tamari, shoyu, or soy sauce

FOR THE SALAD

6 cups baby spinach

2 cups diced cucumber

1 medium carrot, grated

1 tablespoon toasted sesame seeds (optional)

This slightly sweet, gingery dressing is enticingly delicious. I recommend making a big batch of it to have on hand for salads, Asian noodle dishes, and even as an alternative to peanut sauce for Fresh Spring Rolls (page 77). Feel free to vary the vegetables used in the salad as you like, or even top with some edamame or wasabi peas. Please note that different brands of tahini vary in consistency, so if yours is thicker, you may need to add a bit more orange juice.

TO MAKE THE DRESSING

In a large bowl, whisk the tahini and orange juice until smooth. Add the ginger, coconut sugar, and tamari. Whisk well until thoroughly combined.

TO MAKE THE SALAD

In the same bowl as the dressing, combine the spinach, cucumber, and carrot and toss well with the dressing. Serve, topped with the sesame seeds (if using).

Substitution tip: This is also good with other types of greens (baby greens, romaine lettuce, butter lettuce, etc.) in place of the spinach.

Ingredient tip: To toast sesame seeds, place them in a single layer in a dry skillet over low heat. Cook, shaking the pan often, until they're lightly browned and aromatic. This will take under 5 minutes, so watch carefully to avoid burning. Remove from the pan immediately upon toasting.

Per serving: Calories: 170; Fat: 10g; Carbohydrates: 16g; Fiber: 3g; Protein: 9g; Sodium: 318mg; Iron: 7mg

KUCHUMBER

SERVES 3 TO 5

Prep Time: 5 to 10 minutes,
plus 30 minutes for chilling (optional)

- GLUTEN-FREE
- LEFTOVER-FRIENDLY
- NUT-FREE

1 medium cucumber, chopped (1¾ cups)

½ cup halved cherry or grape tomatoes

½ cup chopped red onion

3 tablespoons chopped fresh cilantro

2 tablespoons freshly squeezed lime juice

2 tablespoons sunflower oil

½ teaspoon sea salt

½ teaspoon freshly ground black pepper

This simple, delicious cucumber salad is something you might find me piling onto my plate at an Indian buffet. Its bright, clean flavor works perfectly to balance rich Indian dishes such as the Chickpea Potato Curry (page 165). Serve it on its own or alongside the Indian-Spiced Lemon Rice (page 136) and some Red Lentil Dal (page 108).

In a large bowl, combine the cucumber, tomatoes, red onion, cilantro, lime juice, oil, salt, and pepper. If possible, chill for at least 30 minutes before serving to marry the flavors. Refrigerate leftovers in an airtight container for up to 5 days.

————————

Make it WFPB: Omit the oil and salt and add a tablespoon of water.

Per serving: Calories: 65; Fat: 6g; Carbohydrates: 4g; Fiber: 1g; Protein: 1g; Sodium: 3mg; Iron: 0mg

RAINBOW QUINOA SALAD

SERVES 4

Prep Time: 15 minutes
Cook Time: 15 minutes

○ 30 MINUTES OR LESS
◐ GLUTEN-FREE
● LEFTOVER-FRIENDLY
○ NUT-FREE

3 tablespoons freshly squeezed lime juice

2 tablespoons grated fresh ginger

1½ tablespoons tamari, shoyu, or soy sauce

1 tablespoon toasted sesame oil

1 tablespoon agave nectar

3 medium garlic cloves, minced or pressed

3 cups cooked quinoa (see page 18)

½ cup grated carrot

⅓ cup chopped fresh cilantro

¼ cup minced scallions, both white and green parts

¼ cup corn kernels

¼ cup finely chopped purple cabbage

Don't let the ingredients list fool you—this comes together in less than 20 minutes. Plus, it's the perfect lunch entrée to pack when sandwiches get boring. For an even more salad-like salad, spoon this over baby greens and top with basil microgreens. So pretty and yummy, and so nutrient-dense!

1. In a large bowl, combine the lime juice, ginger, tamari, oil, agave, and garlic and whisk well.

2. Add the cooked quinoa, carrot, cilantro, scallions, corn, and cabbage. Stir until well combined. Refrigerate leftovers in an airtight container for up to 5 days. It's good either warm or cold, but I don't recommend reheating it, as it'll lose much of its freshness if you do.

Make it WFPB: Omit the sesame oil and add ¼ cup toasted sesame seeds to the mixture.

Variation tip: You can simplify the ingredients list by simply using 1 cup of carrots, corn, *or* cabbage (instead of all three). We sometimes do this in a pinch—it's less rainbow-y, but still great.

Per serving: Calories: 238; Fat: 6g; Carbohydrates: 46g; Fiber: 5g; Protein: 7g; Sodium: 418mg; Iron: 9mg

CAULIFLOWER TABBOULEH

SERVES 4

Prep Time: 10 minutes
Cook Time: 10 minutes

○ 30 MINUTES OR LESS
◑ GLUTEN-FREE
● LEFTOVER-FRIENDLY
○ NUT-FREE

2 cups riced cauliflower or 1 (12-ounce) bag frozen cauliflower rice, thawed

¼ cup water

2½ cups minced fresh curly parsley

¾ cup diced cucumber

¼ cup minced fresh mint

½ cup minced red onion

¼ cup plus 2 tablespoons freshly squeezed lemon juice

2 tablespoons extra-virgin olive oil

½ teaspoon sea salt

This all-veggie twist on tabbouleh is delicious, nourishing, and oh-so fresh. It pairs well with Maple Shishitos (page 67), the Garden Collard Wraps (page 122), or even the World's Healthiest Mac and Cheese (page 152). Or, make a lovely light dinner by serving this alongside the Creamy Potato Dill Soup (page 103).

1. In a large skillet or wok, place the cauliflower over medium-high heat. Add the water and cook for 10 minutes, stirring often, until the water is absorbed and the cauliflower is tender. If you need to add more water as you go, do so in small increments. Once tender, set aside to cool.

2. In a large bowl, mix the parsley, cucumber, mint, red onion, lemon juice, olive oil, and salt. Combine thoroughly and add the slightly cooled cauliflower rice. Mix well and serve. Refrigerate leftovers in an airtight container for several days.

Make it WFPB: Omit the oil and substitute water, and omit the salt.

Per serving: Calories: 102; Fat: 5g; Carbohydrates: 9g; Fiber: 3g; Protein: 3g; Sodium: 39mg; Iron: 3mg

BABY GREENS WITH CREAMY DILL DRESSING

SERVES 4

Prep Time: 10 minutes

○ 30 MINUTES OR LESS
● GLUTEN-FREE
○ NUT-FREE

FOR THE CREAMY DILL DRESSING

1 (12-ounce) container firm silken tofu

2 tablespoons apple cider vinegar

1 tablespoon onion granules or powder

¾ teaspoon sea salt

¼ teaspoon freshly ground black pepper

¼ cup minced fresh dill

FOR THE SALAD

8 cups baby greens

1 small cucumber, diced or thinly sliced

½ cup very thin slices red onion (optional)

It's a serious challenge to find a low-fat, oil-free salad dressing that actually tastes satisfying and delicious, which is why I was so darn happy when I came up with this recipe. Plus, it's extremely easy to make—less than 10 minutes for the entire dish. Of course, feel free to add additional vegetables, or a sprinkle of Everything Tofu (page 212) for added sustenance and fun. It's also great with some Red Lentil Potato Soup (page 110) for a light and lovely dinner.

TO MAKE THE CREAMY DILL DRESSING

1. In a blender, combine the tofu, vinegar, onion granules, salt, and pepper and process until completely smooth.

2. Stir in the dill (or blend very briefly—you want to retain the texture of the dill).

TO MAKE THE SALAD

1. In individual bowls, place the greens, cucumber, and onion (if using) and set aside.

2. Pour a generous amount of dressing over each salad and serve immediately.

───────────────

Ingredient tip: Look for silken tofu in the Asian section of health food stores and supermarkets, as it doesn't require refrigeration. It comes in small aseptic packages and is available in soft, firm, and extra-firm. I usually buy the firm, because it makes a thicker dressing and is usually easier to find as an organic version.

Per serving: Calories: 105; Fat: 4g; Carbohydrates: 8g; Fiber: 4g; Protein: 9g; Sodium: 19mg; Iron: 2mg

GINGER LOVER'S KALE SALAD

SERVES 4

Prep Time: 10 minutes

- ○ 30 MINUTES OR LESS
- ◐ GLUTEN-FREE
- ● LEFTOVER-FRIENDLY
- ○ NUT-FREE

6 cups lightly packed kale

2 tablespoons freshly squeezed lime juice

1½ tablespoons maple syrup

1 tablespoon orange juice

1 teaspoon toasted sesame oil

5 medium garlic cloves, pressed or finely minced

1 tablespoon finely grated ginger

¼ teaspoon sea salt

Have you ever gotten kale salad at a restaurant or deli and found it unpleasant to eat? This sad little phenomenon is on my top five all-time pet peeves list. Here's the deal: The texture of raw kale is tough, but can be coaxed into a lovely salad with a few secrets. First of all, you need to start with the right texture (no big stems), then you need an acid to help break down the kale (lime juice in this case), and finally, you need to massage the marinade thoroughly into the kale. Do this, and you'll have a phenomenal kale salad, right in your own kitchen.

1. Remove the stems from the kale and chop the leaves into thin ribbons. Place in a large bowl.

2. Add the lime juice, maple syrup, orange juice, and oil. Use your hands to mix, working the liquids into the kale until it turns a darker shade of green and is softened. This may take a minute, but be patient—well-massaged kale is well worth the effort!

3. Add the garlic, ginger, and salt, and stir well with a spoon until thoroughly combined. This can either be served immediately or refrigerated in an airtight container for up to 5 days. It actually tastes better if you let it marinate in the refrigerator for an hour or more, but I'll understand if you need immediate kale satisfaction.

Make it WFPB: Omit the salt; also omit the sesame oil and substitute extra orange juice.

Per serving: Calories: 50; Fat: 2g; Carbohydrates: 9g; Fiber: 6g; Protein: 1g; Sodium: 18mg; Iron: 1mg

SPINACH ARUGULA SALAD WITH UMEBOSHI SESAME DRESSING

SERVES 4

Prep Time: 5 to 10 minutes

○ 30 MINUTES OR LESS
● GLUTEN-FREE
○ NUT-FREE

4 cups baby arugula

2 cups baby spinach

½ cup finely chopped purple cabbage

2 tablespoons freshly squeezed lime juice

1 tablespoon umeboshi (ume plum) vinegar

1 tablespoon toasted sesame oil

2 tablespoons toasted sesame seeds (see Ingredient tip, page 83)

This salad is the height of simplicity, but is still oh-so delicious. If you're new to the unique flavor of umeboshi, you're in for a surprise. It's salty, tart, and good for digestion. You can find umeboshi vinegar in any health food store and many supermarkets. For a healthy Japanese-inspired feast, serve with Toasted Sesame Sushi with Ginger-Lime Sauce (page 116) and Lemon-Ginger Miso Soup (page 101).

1. In a large bowl, combine the arugula, spinach, and cabbage. Pour the lime juice, vinegar, and oil over the top and mix until very thoroughly combined.

2. Just before serving, sprinkle with the sesame seeds and stir. This is delicious cold or at room temperature.

———————————

Make it WFPB: Omit the oil and substitute an additional ¼ cup toasted sesame seeds instead.

Per serving: Calories: 83; Fat: 7g; Carbohydrates: 4g; Fiber: 2g; Protein: 2g; Sodium: 335mg; Iron: 2mg

VEGAN COBB SALAD

SERVES 4

Prep Time: 5 minutes

 GLUTEN-FREE

○ PLAN AHEAD

2 heads romaine lettuce, chopped

Everything Tofu (page 212)

2 avocados, chopped

1½ cups cherry or grape tomatoes

¼ small red onion, very thinly sliced

1 cup Cashew Ranch Dressing (page 205)

There's something so decadent about a good Cobb salad. A meal unto itself, this salad is both simple in construction and complex in flavor. It's also delicious alongside a light soup such as the Very Vegetable Soup (page 104) or Lemon-Ginger Miso Soup (page 101).

Into individual bowls, place the romaine lettuce and top evenly with the tofu, avocados, tomatoes, and onion. Top with the Cashew Ranch Dressing and enjoy immediately.

———————————

Make it WFPB: Simply omit the oil in the Everything Tofu if you'd like to keep this oil-free. Easy peasy!

Meal prep it: If you love this salad, be sure to keep the Cashew Ranch Dressing on hand (or make up a double batch), and have your tofu ready to go as well. The tofu is great fresh out of the oven, but it's also delicious as a cold element from the refrigerator.

Per serving: Calories: 552; Fat: 37g; Carbohydrates: 35g; Fiber: 15g; Protein: 31g; Sodium: 585mg; Iron: 8mg

SHIITAKE, WALNUT, AND CHERRY SALAD

SERVES 4

Prep Time: 10 minutes
Cook Time: 5 minutes

○ 30 MINUTES OR LESS
● GLUTEN-FREE

1½ tablespoons extra-virgin olive oil, divided

1 cup sliced shiitake mushrooms

4 medium garlic cloves, minced or pressed

½ cup very thinly sliced red onion

¼ cup dried cherries

3 tablespoons balsamic vinegar

1 tablespoon pure maple syrup

2 teaspoons orange zest

½ teaspoon sea salt

¼ teaspoon freshly ground black pepper

6 cups mixed baby greens

¼ cup chopped walnuts or walnut pieces

This salad is a celebration of one of my very favorite fungi, the shiitake mushroom. Shiitakes are incredibly immune-boosting, and sautéing them lightly is a great way to bring out their beautiful, complex flavor. I love this salad alongside the Creamy Potato Dill Soup (page 103) or some Simple Staple Rice (page 134) for a tasty yet uncomplicated meal.

1. In a medium skillet, heat 1 teaspoon of oil over medium-high heat and sauté the mushrooms and garlic for 5 minutes, or until the mushrooms are lightly browned and tender. Remove from heat and set aside.

2. In a large bowl, add the remaining oil, onion, cherries, vinegar, maple syrup, orange zest, salt, and pepper. Stir well. Add the greens and the shiitake mixture and stir thoroughly. Serve sprinkled with the walnuts.

Make it WFPB: Sauté the mushrooms and garlic in water. Replace the oil in the dressing with orange juice, and omit the salt.

Per serving: Calories: 186; Fat: 8g; Carbohydrates: 22g; Fiber: 2g; Protein: 3g; Sodium: 20mg; Iron: 1mg

12 TREASURES SALAD

SERVES 4 TO 6

Prep Time: 10 minutes, plus marinating time

○ 30 MINUTES OR LESS
◐ GLUTEN-FREE
● LEFTOVER-FRIENDLY
○ NUT-FREE

1 (15-ounce) can black beans, drained and rinsed, or 1½ cups cooked black beans (see page 17)

½ cup chopped dried apricots

½ cup mango juice

½ cup chopped fresh cilantro

½ cup corn kernels

2 scallions, both green and white parts, trimmed and minced

2 large garlic cloves, minced or pressed

2 tablespoons neutral-flavored oil (such as sunflower or avocado)

2 tablespoons freshly squeezed lime juice

½ tablespoon grated fresh ginger

¾ teaspoon sea salt

5 cups chopped baby spinach

I think of this salad as a bowl full of treasures—and to me, the marinated dried apricot pieces look like little jewels. I've been making variations of this salad for decades, as it's so tasty and perfect for when you want vegetables to be the main dish. Serve this with a little quinoa or Simple Staple Rice (page 134) for a healthy, satisfying meal. It's also delicious alongside the Very Vegetable Soup (page 104) or Red Lentil Potato Soup (page 110).

1. In a large airtight container, mix the beans, apricots, mango juice, cilantro, corn, scallions, garlic, oil, lime juice, ginger, and salt. Stir very well. Marinate for at least 1 hour, or up to 2 days, in the refrigerator.

2. Bring the salad to room temperature and toss with the spinach. Serve. Refrigerate leftovers in an airtight container for up to 5 days.

_____

Make it WFPB: Replace the oil with additional mango juice and omit the salt.

Substitution tip: Feel free to use minced red or orange pepper, shelled edamame, or a combination of the two in place of the corn kernels.

Per serving: Calories: 163; Fat: 5g; Carbohydrates: 25g; Fiber: 6g; Protein: 5g; Sodium: 53mg; Iron: 5mg

ROMAINE SALAD WITH MAGICAL GINGER DRESSING

SERVES 6

Prep Time: 10 minutes

- ○ 30 MINUTES OR LESS
- ● GLUTEN-FREE
- ○ NUT-FREE

FOR THE MAGICAL GINGER DRESSING

⅓ cup chopped white or yellow onion

¼ cup fresh lime juice

3 tablespoons grated fresh ginger

2 tablespoons minced celery

3 large garlic cloves, peeled

1 tablespoon tomato paste

1 tablespoon coconut sugar

¼ cup water

½ cup oil (light olive, sunflower, or avocado)

½ teaspoon freshly ground black pepper

1¼ teaspoons sea salt

FOR THE SALAD

2 heads romaine lettuce, chopped

2 large tomatoes, chopped

1 cup shelled edamame, thawed if frozen

This rosy-colored dressing has a bright, enticing flavor and pairs perfectly with crispy romaine, tomatoes, and edamame. This recipe is an updated version of a dressing I created decades ago and has a special place in my heart, because my daughter's best childhood friend used to be so obsessed with it that her mother could get her to eat anything as long as this dressing was on top.

TO MAKE THE MAGICAL GINGER DRESSING

1. In a blender, combine the onion, lime juice, ginger, celery, garlic, tomato paste, and sugar. Blend until all of the chunky items have become emulsified. If needed, add a little of the water, starting with a tablespoon at a time, to make your blender cooperate.

2. Add the remaining water, oil, pepper, and salt and blend until totally smooth.

TO MAKE THE SALAD

1. In individual bowls, divide the lettuce, tomatoes, and edamame and set aside.

2. Pour the desired amount of dressing over the salads and enjoy immediately.

Batch cooking tip: The dressing recipe makes more than you'll need for the salad, but that's how I like to do food prep at my house—it's always so nice to have extra sauces and dressings on hand throughout the week, so that meals can come together quickly. Refrigerate the dressing in an airtight container for up to 2 weeks, and use on salads, rice, noodles, or bean dishes.

Make it WFPB: Omit the oil and add ¼ cup soaked and drained cashews (page 11) into the dressing, along with ½ cup water. Blend until very smooth with the remaining ingredients. Omit the salt.

Per serving (Salad + ¼ cup dressing): Calories: 232; Fat: 20g; Carbohydrates: 13g; Fiber: 6g; Protein: 4g; Sodium: 41mg; Iron: 2mg

TESS'S TACO SALAD

SERVES 4

Prep Time: 20 minutes

Cook Time: About 15 minutes

● GLUTEN-FREE
○ NUT-FREE
● PLAN AHEAD

FOR THE CHIPS

8 corn tortillas (preferably sprouted)

Nonstick cooking spray (olive or coconut oil)

FOR THE SALAD

1 (15-ounce) can fat-free vegan refried beans

2 heads romaine lettuce, finely chopped

1 cup finely chopped purple cabbage

Cauliflower Taco Meat (page 213)

1 cup Avotillo Sauce (page 201), Cheesy Sauce (page 210), or Low-Fat Cheese Dip (page 208)

1 cup Classic Salsa (page 202) or store-bought salsa

Make it WFPB: Omit the oil spray for the chips and use the WFPB recommendations for the Cauliflower Taco Meat.

Per serving: Calories: 355; Fat: 9g; Carbohydrates: 59g; Fiber: 18g; Protein: 17g; Sodium: 1203mg; Iron: 7mg

I was so bold as to name this salad after myself, because it's one of those go-to staples I just love and never get sick of. I also love how customizable it is—any of the sauces will work beautifully here, and you can also add different types of vegetables or lettuces if you like. I also enjoy this with the Walnut-Quinoa Crumbles (page 124) as a variation sometimes. Plus, it's just so fun to eat any food that you can scoop with chips. If you're like me and air-fry everything, feel free to use an air fryer instead of the oven for your chips (they'll cook in about half the time).

TO MAKE THE CHIPS

1. Preheat the oven to 400°F.

2. Cut the tortillas into quarters. On a large nonstick or silicone-lined baking sheet, place the tortillas in a single layer. Spray the tops lightly with oil and bake for 5 minutes. Remove from the oven, flip each chip over, spray again, and bake for another 3 to 5 minutes. If any are lightly browned at this point, remove them. If needed, bake for another 3 to 5 minutes. Be sure to check them often, as they can burn quickly. Once lightly browned, remove and set aside.

TO MAKE THE SALAD

1. In a small pot, heat the refried beans over medium-low heat. If needed, add a little water to thin. Stir often and remove once hot.

2. Place the lettuce and cabbage in bowls and toss well. Top evenly with the beans, Cauliflower Taco Meat, Avotillo Sauce, and Classic Salsa. Serve with chips for dipping.

Soothing Miso Ramen Soup, page 102

SOUPS AND STEWS

CHICKY NOODLE SOUP

SERVES 4 TO 6

Prep Time: 5 minutes

Cook Time: 10 minutes

○ 30 MINUTES OR LESS
● GLUTEN-FREE
○ NUT-FREE
● PLAN AHEAD

8 cups water

2 cups brown rice rotini noodles

1 (15-ounce) can chickpeas, drained and rinsed, or 1½ cups cooked chickpeas (see page 17)

½ cup Chicky Seasoning (page 198)

½ cup diced carrots

½ cup diced celery

4 large garlic cloves, minced or pressed

I adore this soup. It's oil-free—yet richly satisfying—and overflowing with nutrients, fiber, and immune-boosting properties. Plus, I always seem to have the ingredients on hand, so I often turn to this when I need something comforting and nutrient-dense in a pinch. For a get-better-soon meal, serve this with Ginger-Glazed Bok Choy (page 69) or some Ginger Lover's Kale Salad (page 89).

1. In a large pot, combine the water, noodles, chickpeas, Chicky Seasoning, carrots, celery, and garlic and bring to a boil over high heat, stirring well.

2. Reduce the heat to low and simmer for 10 minutes, or until the noodles are al dente. Be sure not to cook the noodles until totally soft, as they'll soften a bit more as they sit in the hot soup. Serve immediately.

———————————

Meal prep it: This doesn't store as well as other varieties of soup, since the noodles can become mushy when stored for longer periods of time. However, if you keep the seasoning on hand, as well as diced carrots and celery, this will come together quicker.

Make it WFPB: Omit the salt from the seasoning.

Per serving: Calories: 257; Fat: 3g; Carbohydrates: 45g; Fiber: 6g; Protein: 10g; Sodium: 151mg; Iron: 3mg

LEMON-GINGER MISO SOUP

SERVES 4

Prep Time: 3 to 5 minutes

Cook Time: 2 to 3 minutes

○ 30 MINUTES OR LESS
◉ GLUTEN-FREE
○ NUT-FREE

¼ cup plus 2 tablespoons white miso

3 cups water, divided

3½ tablespoons freshly squeezed lemon juice

2 tablespoons grated fresh ginger

2½ teaspoons tamari, shoyu, or soy sauce

1 teaspoon toasted sesame oil

¼ cup finely chopped chives or scallions

This simple soup is great for boosting the immune system, thanks to the ginger, lemon, and miso. It's also very flavorful and comforting and is great served with some Toasted Sesame Sushi with Ginger-Lime Sauce (page 116), or warm whole-grain bread. For extra flair and color contrast, you can top this with black sesame seeds.

1. In a medium soup pot, combine the miso with 2 to 3 tablespoons of the water. Whisk until smooth.

2. Add the remaining water, lemon juice, ginger, tamari, and sesame oil. Set to low heat. Cook for 2 to 3 minutes, stirring often, just until the soup is nicely warmed (do not boil). Top with the chives and serve immediately.

Ingredient tip: Be sure not to boil miso soup at any point, as excess heat can destroy miso's nutritional properties. Also, resist the temptation to use red miso instead of the mellow white miso, as it won't fit as well with this recipe's delicate flavor profile.

Make it WFPB: Omit the toasted sesame oil and top with 2 tablespoons toasted sesame seeds instead.

Per serving: Calories: 70; Fat: 2g; Carbohydrates: 8g; Fiber: 2g; Protein: 4g; Sodium: 1172mg; Iron: 1mg

SOOTHING MISO RAMEN SOUP

SERVES 4

Prep Time: 10 minutes

Cook Time: 10 minutes (depending on your vegetables of choice)

- ○ 30 MINUTES OR LESS
- ◑ GLUTEN-FREE
- ● LEFTOVER-FRIENDLY
- ○ NUT-FREE
- ◑ PLAN AHEAD

4¼ cups water, divided

¼ cup unsalted roasted sunflower seeds

¼ cup white miso

2 tablespoons Chicky Seasoning (page 198)

5 large garlic cloves, peeled

1 tablespoon tamari, shoyu, or soy sauce

4 cups vegetables of choice, uniformly chopped or sliced

4 nests (70g each) ramen noodles

Meal prep it: To guarantee many bowls of happiness over the week, make a batch (or double batch) of the broth and store it in the refrigerator in an airtight container. You can also keep the veggies cut up and ready to stir-fry for extra ease.

Ingredient tip: I am always careful not to boil miso, as it can destroy some of its beneficial nutrients. When reheating, warm over low heat until warm or hot, but not boiling.

Per serving: Calories: 408; Fat: 5g; Carbohydrates: 72g; Fiber: 11g; Protein: 21g; Sodium: 1554mg; Iron: 7mg

This comforting, nutrient-dense soup makes for a light yet delicious feast when served alongside the Romaine Salad with Magical Ginger Dressing (page 95) or the Spinach Salad with Sesame-Ginger-Orange Dressing (page 83). To really take it up a notch, add some Fresh Spring Rolls with Peanut Sauce (page 77) on the side. You can also enjoy it topped with some nori or toasted sesame seeds for extra crunch. I recommend using brown rice and millet ramen noodles.

1. In a blender, combine 4 cups water, sunflower seeds, miso, Chicky Seasoning, garlic, and tamari, and process until very smooth. Set aside. (At this point, you can also refrigerate this broth for up to 2 weeks.)

2. In a large skillet or wok, stir-fry the vegetables in about ¼ cup water (or a tablespoon of sesame oil, if you prefer) over high heat, until tender but still slightly crisp. It will take 5 to 10 minutes, depending on what vegetables you use. I like sliced shiitake mushrooms, thinly sliced carrots, chopped scallions, and baby bok choy.

3. While the vegetables are cooking, boil a pot of water and cook the noodles according to the directions on the package.

4. To assemble, ladle the broth into bowls and top with ramen and vegetables. Enjoy immediately.

CREAMY POTATO DILL SOUP

SERVES 6 TO 8

Prep Time: 5 minutes
Cook Time: 20 to 25 minutes

- ○ GLUTEN-FREE
- ● LEFTOVER-FRIENDLY
- ○ PLAN AHEAD

7 cups water, divided

5 cups chopped red or gold potatoes

1 (15-ounce) can navy beans, rinsed and drained, or 1½ cups cooked navy beans (see page 17)

1 cup raw unsalted whole cashews, soaked, drained, and rinsed (see page 11)

¼ cup minced fresh dill

5 large garlic cloves, minced or pressed

1¾ teaspoons sea salt

¼ teaspoon ground white pepper

¼ teaspoon freshly ground black pepper

Ingredient tip: Most people peel their potatoes for soups and other dishes, but I love keeping the skins on for two big reasons: 1) It's less work. How a-*peeling* is that? 2) You always get more nutrients from food when you leave the skins on—many important nutrients in whole plant-based foods are located just under (or in) the skin.

Per serving: Calories: 231; Fat: 6g; Carbohydrates: 43g; Fiber: 15g; Protein: 16g; Sodium: 2mg; Iron: 5mg

I'd been wanting to create the perfect creamy potato soup for years—one that was both delicious and made from whole foods—and one night, it finally happened. I was grilling out with my family on a warm fall evening and felt like we needed a little something to go along with our veggies to make the meal more substantial. Luckily, this soup was the perfect solution, and even our picky teenagers devoured it. As any parent knows, that's a great feeling. You can serve this luscious, nutritious soup with grilled or roasted vegetables as we did, but it's also delightful alongside the Vegan Cobb Salad (page 91).

1. In a large pot, combine 6 cups water and the potatoes and bring to a boil over high heat. Reduce the heat to low and simmer for 20 to 25 minutes, or until potatoes are very tender.

2. While the potatoes are cooking, in a blender, combine the beans, cashews, and remaining 1 cup water and blend until velvety smooth. Set aside.

3. Once the potatoes are tender, turn off the heat and mash the potatoes in the pot using a potato masher or fork, until only small chunks remain.

4. Stir the cashew-bean purée into the soup. Add the dill, garlic, salt, white pepper, and black pepper to the soup. Stir well. If necessary, warm briefly on low heat until the soup is the desired temperature. Serve immediately. Refrigerate leftovers in an airtight container for up to a week.

VERY VEGETABLE SOUP

SERVES 4 TO 6

Prep Time: 5 minutes
Cook Time: 45 minutes

- ● GLUTEN-FREE
- ● LEFTOVER-FRIENDLY
- ○ NUT-FREE

5 cups water

1 (14.5-ounce) can diced tomatoes

1 (15-ounce) can tomato sauce

2 large celery stalks, diced (1¼ cups)

2 medium carrots, diced (1 cup)

½ medium white or yellow onion, diced (½ cup)

1 cup peas

1 cup corn kernels

3 large garlic cloves, minced or pressed

1 teaspoon freshly ground black pepper

½ teaspoon salt

This soup is all about the veggies. It's very clean, very light, very tasty, and very high in fiber—yet devoid of excess fats, sugars, and fillers. It's great on its own or served with whole-grain bread or crackers. For a light, tasty meal bursting with vegetables, serve this with the Arugula Salad with Miso-Goji Dressing (page 82) or some Kuchumber (page 84). Incidentally, this is not just a favorite in our house—my recipe testers adored this soup, too!

1. In a large pot, combine the water, tomatoes and their juices, tomato sauce, celery, carrots, and onion over medium-high heat. Bring to a boil. Reduce the heat to low and simmer, uncovered, for 35 minutes, stirring occasionally.

2. Add the peas, corn, garlic, pepper, and salt. Stir and continue to cook for another 10 minutes, or until the vegetables are tender but still slightly crisp, and the soup has thickened slightly. Serve hot or warm. Refrigerate leftovers in an airtight container for up to a week or freeze for several months.

Variation tip: To give this soup a wintry twist, swap the corn and peas for kale and cooked barley (pictured). It will thicken the soup significantly, giving it a fuller, entrée feel.

Per serving: Calories: 91; Fat: 1g; Carbohydrates: 19g; Fiber: 5g; Protein: 4g; Sodium: 567mg; Iron: 1mg

TEMPEH CORN CHILI

SERVES 6 TO 8

Prep Time: 10 minutes
Cook Time: 30 to 45 minutes

- GLUTEN-FREE
- ● LEFTOVER-FRIENDLY
- ○ NUT-FREE
- PLAN AHEAD

2 tablespoons oil (olive, sunflower, or avocado), divided

8 ounces crumbled tempeh (2 cups)

2 small white or yellow onions, finely chopped

2 (14.5-ounce) cans diced tomatoes

2½ cups water

1 (15-ounce) can kidney beans, drained and rinsed, or 1½ cups cooked kidney beans (see page 17)

1½ cups corn kernels

¼ cup plus 2 tablespoons tamari, shoyu, or soy sauce

6 tablespoons salt-free chili powder

7 large garlic cloves, minced or pressed

2 tablespoons Chicky Seasoning (page 198)

2 tablespoons coconut sugar

2 tablespoons balsamic vinegar

2 teaspoons sea salt

This soul-satisfying chili will please even the most dedicated meat-eaters, as well as hungry vegans. I've been making variations of it for decades and have yet to find anyone who doesn't a) love this, b) request seconds, and c) ask for the recipe. This is especially good served with some cornbread or whole-grain bread on the side.

1. In a large soup pot, heat 1 teaspoon of the oil and the crumbled tempeh. Cook for 2 to 3 minutes, stirring often, until lightly browned. If necessary, add a little water to prevent the tempeh from sticking.

2. Add the remaining 1 tablespoon oil and the onions. Sauté for 3 to 5 minutes, or until the onions begin to soften and brown a bit. If necessary, add a little of the water to prevent sticking.

3. Stir in the tomatoes and their juices, water, beans, corn, tamari, chili powder, garlic, Chicky Seasoning, coconut sugar, and vinegar. Stir well and reduce heat to medium-low. Simmer, stirring often, for 30 to 45 minutes, or until thickened.

4. Stir in the salt and serve hot or warm. Refrigerate leftovers in an airtight container for up to week.

Make it WFPB: Replace the oil with water or vegetable broth and omit the salt.

Per serving: Calories: 240; Fat: 6g; Carbohydrates: 30g; Fiber: 6g; Protein: 14g; Sodium: 1081mg; Iron: 3mg

QUICK CURRIED CABBAGE

SERVES 4

Prep Time: 5 to 10 minutes

Cook Time: 10 minutes

○ 30 MINUTES OR LESS
◐ GLUTEN-FREE
● LEFTOVER-FRIENDLY
○ NUT-FREE

2 teaspoons sunflower or coconut oil

1 teaspoon ground cumin

1 teaspoon ground coriander

½ teaspoon ground turmeric

6 cups chopped green cabbage

½ cup water

20 small curry leaves (optional)

1 tablespoon freshly squeezed lime juice

2 large garlic cloves, minced or pressed

¾ teaspoon salt

Does it make me a weirdo to get ridiculously excited about a big bowl of curried cabbage that can be made in under 10 minutes? Maybe. But it's the simple things sometimes, right? If you want to make this delicious dish part of a healthy feast, it's great alongside the Indian-Spiced Lemon Rice (page 136) and Red Lentil Dal (page 108).

1. In a large skillet or wok, combine the oil, cumin, coriander, and turmeric over medium-high heat. Stir-fry the spices for 1 minute.

2. Add the cabbage and stir well. Add the water, curry leaves (if using), lime juice, and garlic. Cook for another 9 minutes, stirring often, until the cabbage is wilted and all of the water has been absorbed. Season with salt and serve. Refrigerate in an airtight container for up to 5 days.

———————————————

Make it WFPB: Omit step 1 and simply stir-fry the cumin, coriander, turmeric, cabbage, water, curry leaves, lime juice, and garlic until soft, about 9 minutes. If necessary, add more water to keep from sticking. Skip the salt at the end and serve immediately.

Per serving: Calories: 57; Fat: 4g; Carbohydrates: 2g; Fiber: 15g; Protein: 0g; Sodium: 1mg; Iron: 0mg

RED LENTIL DAL

SERVES 8

Prep Time: 5 minutes
Cook Time: About 50 minutes

● GLUTEN-FREE
● LEFTOVER-FRIENDLY
○ NUT-FREE

10 cups water

2 cups red lentils

3 tablespoons minced fresh ginger

2 tablespoons cumin seeds

1 tablespoon ground coriander

1 teaspoon ground turmeric

½ teaspoon red pepper flakes

30 curry leaves (optional)

½ cup chopped fresh cilantro

5 large garlic cloves, minced or pressed

1 tablespoon coconut oil (extra-virgin is ideal, as it adds some coconut flavor)

2 teaspoons sea salt

There's something so heavenly about a bowl of warm, fresh dal. It's a go-to dish for me (and my daughter) at vegan-friendly Indian restaurants and is delicious plain or with a little rice spooned in. This is the perfect counterpart for Chickpea Potato Curry (page 165) with some Kuchumber (page 84) on the side.

1. In a large pot, combine the water and lentils and stir well. Add the ginger, cumin, coriander, turmeric, red pepper flakes, and curry leaves (if using). Bring to a boil over high heat. Reduce the heat to low and simmer, uncovered, for 45 minutes, or until the dahl is thick and the lentils are very tender. Stir every 10 minutes or so.

2. Remove from the heat and stir in the cilantro, garlic, oil, and salt. Stir well and serve. There is no need to remove the curry leaves, because they're edible. Refrigerate leftovers in an airtight container for up to a week.

Ingredient tip: Despite all of the tips online about the "best way to peel fresh ginger," there is actually no need to peel the ginger at all. Many of its important nutrients are located in and under the skin. Not to mention, peeling it just creates unnecessary work. Instead, simply wash your ginger well and cut off any especially rough-looking parts. Then, mince it up, skin and all.

Per serving: Calories: 147; Fat: 2g; Carbohydrates: 24g; Fiber: 5g; Protein: 8g; Sodium: 4mg; Iron: 4mg

CREAMY DREAMY LENTILS

SERVES 4 TO 6

Prep Time: 5 minutes
Cook Time: 45 to 55 minutes

- GLUTEN-FREE
- LEFTOVER-FRIENDLY
- NUT-FREE

2 cups water

1 (14.5-ounce) can diced tomatoes

1 (13.5-ounce) can full-fat coconut milk

1½ cups brown or green lentils

½ cup diced white or yellow onion

2½ teaspoons ground cumin

¼ cup freshly squeezed lemon juice

2 tablespoons creamy peanut butter

4 large garlic cloves, pressed or minced

2 teaspoons sea salt

These rich and luscious lentils are pure comfort on a cold evening. For a complete meal, I recommend serving them with some whole-grain bread for sopping up the sauce and a salad, such as the Spinach Arugula Salad with Umeboshi Sesame Dressing (page 90). Incidentally, if you're looking for a great (yet easy to make) potluck dish, you've found it. This recipe is easy to double (or triple), and it never fails to impress.

1. In a large pot, bring the water, tomatoes and their juices, coconut milk, lentils, onion, and cumin to a boil over medium-high heat.

2. Reduce the heat to low and simmer, partially covered, stirring occasionally, for 45 to 55 minutes, or until the lentils are very tender. All of the liquid probably won't absorb (this is a saucy dish), so just cook until the lentils are very soft.

3. In a large bowl, whisk the lemon juice, peanut butter, garlic, and salt together until smooth. Stir in the lentil mixture and serve. Refrigerate leftovers in an airtight container for up to a week.

Substitution tip: If you prefer, substitute mung beans for the lentils and cook them for an additional 20 minutes, or until softened.

Per serving: Calories: 255; Fat: 13g; Carbohydrates: 26g; Fiber: 6g; Protein: 9g; Sodium: 153mg; Iron: 3mg

RED LENTIL POTATO SOUP

SERVES 4 TO 6

Prep Time: 5 minutes

Cook Time: About 25 minutes

○ 30 MINUTES OR LESS
◐ GLUTEN-FREE
● LEFTOVER-FRIENDLY
○ NUT-FREE
◐ PLAN AHEAD

7 cups water

2½ cups unpeeled russet or gold potatoes, diced into ½-inch cubes

1½ cups red lentils

1 large carrot, chopped (¾ cup)

¼ cup Chicky Seasoning (page 198)

1 tablespoon dried rosemary leaf

4 large garlic cloves, minced or pressed

1 teaspoon sea salt

½ teaspoon freshly ground black pepper

This is *the* soup at our house (especially if you ask my daughter). If you keep the Chicky Seasoning (page 198) on hand at all times (like any law-abiding citizen should), it's a snap to make. For a delicious, oil-free meal, serve this with Baby Greens with Creamy Dill Dressing (page 88) and some Mint Chocolate Chip Nice Cream (page 180) for dessert.

1. In a large pot, combine the water, potatoes, lentils, carrot, Chicky Seasoning, and rosemary and stir well. Bring to a boil.

2. Reduce the heat to low and simmer, uncovered, for 25 minutes, or until the potatoes are tender, the red lentils are very soft, and the soup is thickened. Stir often.

3. Remove from the heat and stir in the garlic, salt, and pepper. Serve hot or warm. Refrigerate leftovers in an airtight container for up to a week.

_____

Variation tip: You can also blend this soup if you'd like a smooth, velvety result (pictured). Once you've finished cooking the soup and have added the salt, pepper, and garlic, either use an immersion blender or place the soup in a blender and blend until smooth. If you'd like, add a dollop of Cashew-Macadamia Cheese (page 204) on top for an extra treat.

Per serving: Calories: 156; Fat: 0g; Carbohydrates: 29g; Fiber: 6g; Protein: 10g; Sodium: 48mg; Iron: 3mg

MULLIGATAWNY

SERVES 8

Prep Time: 10 minutes
Cook Time: 35 minutes

⬤ GLUTEN-FREE
⬤ LEFTOVER-FRIENDLY

4 cups water

1¼ cups red lentils

2 teaspoons cumin seeds

2¼ cups full-fat coconut milk

1¼ cups chopped fresh cilantro, divided

¾ cup freshly squeezed lemon juice

8 large garlic cloves, peeled

1 tablespoon sea salt

1 teaspoon freshly ground black pepper

½ teaspoon asafetida powder

George Costanza would have waited in line all day for this soup—it's that good. Serve this luscious soup with warm bread or some of the Simple Staple Rice (page 134) and the Ginger Lover's Kale Salad (page 89) for a great meal.

1. In a large pot, bring the water, lentils, and cumin seeds to a boil over medium-high heat. Partially cover the pot with a lid, allowing steam to escape. Reduce the heat to low and simmer for 25 to 35 minutes, until the lentils are very soft. Allow to cool slightly.

2. In a blender, combine the coconut milk, 1 cup cilantro, lemon juice, garlic, salt, pepper, and asafetida until smooth.

3. Add the cooked lentils and blend until velvety smooth. Serve warm, topped with the remaining ¼ cup chopped cilantro.

_____

First-timer tip: If you have any leftover soup, store refrigerated in an airtight container for up to 5 days. However, it will thicken considerably after being refrigerated, so you'll want to thin it with a little water or coconut milk upon reheating it.

Ingredient tip: Find asafetida in Indian grocery stores, international supermarkets, or online.

Per serving: Calories: 192; Fat: 10g; Carbohydrates: 18g; Fiber: 3g; Protein: 6g; Sodium: 28mg; Iron: 2mg

ETHIOPIAN-SPICED YELLOW SPLIT PEAS

SERVES 6

Prep Time: 5 minutes
Cook Time: 40 minutes

● GLUTEN-FREE
● LEFTOVER-FRIENDLY
○ NUT-FREE

6 cups water

1½ cups dry yellow split peas

1 tablespoon coconut oil

1 tablespoon berbere

1 tablespoon minced fresh ginger

4 medium garlic cloves, minced or pressed

½ teaspoon ground turmeric

1 teaspoon sea salt

Also known as *Yekik Alicha*, this Ethiopian-inspired dish is comfort in a bowl. If you have access to (or know how to make) the flatbread injera, serve it with that, as it's the most traditional (and delicious) option. Otherwise, you can serve these saucy lentils with warm tortillas, pita wedges, or brown rice. Or, use this to make one of my all-time favorite snacks, Yellow Split Pea Rolls with Berbere Sauce (page 76).

1. In a large pot, combine the water and split peas over medium heat. Bring to a boil, then reduce the heat to medium-low and simmer for about 10 minutes.

2. Stir in the oil, berbere, ginger, garlic, and turmeric. Cook over medium-low heat for about 30 minutes, stirring often, until all liquids are absorbed and the peas are tender. If the mixture becomes dry before the peas are tender, stir in a little more water as you go.

3. Stir in the salt and serve warm or hot. Refrigerate leftovers in an airtight container for up to a week. When you reheat this, you'll likely need to add more water as it will thicken upon storage.

Ingredient tip: Berbere is a traditional Ethiopian spice blend available online, in Ethiopian restaurants, and in specialty or international markets.

Make it WFPB: Substitute extra water for the oil and omit the salt.

Per serving: Calories: 192; Fat: 10g; Carbohydrates: 18g; Fiber: 3g; Protein: 6g; Sodium: 28mg; Iron: 2mg

SOUPS AND STEWS

Toasted Sesame Sushi with
Ginger-Lime Sauce, page 116

CHAPTER EIGHT

HANDHELDS

TOASTED SESAME SUSHI WITH GINGER-LIME SAUCE

SERVES 4

Prep Time: 20 minutes
Cook Time: About 50 minutes

● GLUTEN-FREE
○ NUT-FREE
◐ WFPB

1 cup short-grain brown rice

3 cups water

2 tablespoons freshly squeezed lime juice

2 tablespoons tamari, shoyu, or soy sauce

2 teaspoons grated fresh ginger

2 tablespoons sesame seeds

½ just-ripe avocado, thinly sliced

½ small cucumber (½ cup), julienned

4 nori sheets, raw or toasted

Ingredient tip: Did you know you don't have to peel ginger? Simply wash your ginger root well and remove any gnarly parts. Then, grate it using a fine grater (don't waste your money on a ginger grater—most just sit there and look cute).

Per serving: Calories: 217; Fat: 6g; Carbohydrates: 40g; Fiber: 6g; Protein: 6g; Sodium: 507mg; Iron: 2mg

Sushi is the ultimate handheld—especially for people like me who are embarrassingly awkward with chopsticks. I love this recipe because it's so clean, light, full of nutrient-dense superfoods, and yet so fun to eat.

1. Cook the rice in the water according to the instructions on page 18. Once cooked, remove from heat, uncover, and fluff with a fork. Allow to cool slightly, stirring occasionally to allow steam to escape.

2. While the rice is cooking, in a small bowl, stir the lime juice, tamari, and ginger together and set aside.

3. In a dry pan, toast the sesame seeds over low heat for 4 to 5 minutes, or until lightly browned and aromatic. Shake the pan occasionally so they cook evenly. Remove from heat.

4. Place a nori sheet on the counter, shiny-side down. Distribute one-quarter of the rice over the lower half of the nori sheet and press down evenly. You may like to dip your hands in a bowl of water from time to time so the rice doesn't stick. Sprinkle the toasted sesame seeds on top of the rice and press them down.

5. Create a horizontal groove along the middle of the rice (parallel to the nori) and fill with one-quarter of the avocado and cucumber.

6. To roll, bring the bottom of the nori up and over the rice and toppings. Tuck well, gently squeezing so that the toppings and rice are secure inside the nori.

7. With water, moisten the top edge of the nori and roll the rest of the way up. Place the roll seal-side down until it's ready to slice. Repeat with the other rolls.

8. To cut, wet a very sharp knife and slice each roll into 1-inch pieces. Serve drizzled with the sauce.

CHICKY TEMPEH WRAPS

SERVES 4

Prep Time: 10 minutes

Cook Time: 10 minutes

- GLUTEN-FREE
- LEFTOVER-FRIENDLY
- PLAN AHEAD

8 ounces tempeh, cut into 1-inch cubes

½ cup water

1 tablespoon tamari, shoyu, or soy sauce

1 tablespoon Chicky Seasoning (page 198) (optional)

2 large garlic cloves, minced or pressed

4 large whole-grain or brown rice tortillas

½ cup Cashew Ranch Dressing (page 205) or Cashew-Macadamia Cheese (page 204)

4 large leaves romaine or red leaf lettuce, for serving

¼ cup thinly sliced red onion, for serving

1 medium tomato, chopped, for serving

¼ cup chopped or sliced pickles, for serving

These wraps are super simple and satisfying, so I tend to rely on them regularly. Feel free to get creative with variations—if you don't have the dressing or cheese on hand, substitute ketchup and Dijon mustard, or another sauce of your choice. For a Mexican flair, use guacamole and season the tempeh with chili powder instead of the Chicky Seasoning (pair the tempeh with some fajita-style veggies in place of the raw vegetables). Have fun finding your favorite version of this wrap.

1. In a large skillet or wok, heat the tempeh and water over medium-high heat. Lightly steam the tempeh, covered, for 1 to 2 minutes.

2. Uncover and sprinkle with the tamari, Chicky Seasoning (if using), and garlic. Cook, stirring gently and often, for 4 to 5 minutes, until the tempeh is hot and lightly browned. Remove from heat and set aside.

3. In a large skillet, warm the tortillas over medium-high heat for up to 1 minute per side, until just heated through.

4. To assemble, divide the tempeh evenly between the tortillas. Drizzle the Cashew Ranch Dressing over the tempeh and top with lettuce, onion, tomato, and/or pickles. Serve immediately.

Meal prep it: The tempeh, once cooked, will keep in an airtight container in the refrigerator for up to a week. If you keep that and the dressing or cheese on hand, these will come together in under 5 minutes.

Make it WFPB: Omit the salt from the seasoning, ranch dressing, and cheese.

Per serving: Calories: 229; Fat: 9g; Carbohydrates: 26g; Fiber: 4g; Protein: 12g; Sodium: 370mg; Iron: 2mg

DILLY TOFU SALAD WRAPS

SERVES 4

Prep Time: 15 minutes

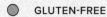 GLUTEN-FREE
PLAN AHEAD

FOR THE DILLY TOFU SALAD

8 ounces firm tofu

1 medium carrot, grated (½ cup)

¼ cup plus 2 tablespoons Cashew Ranch Dressing (page 205)

¼ cup diced red bell pepper

¼ cup minced dill pickle

2 tablespoons minced red, yellow, or white onion

2 medium garlic cloves, minced or pressed

2 teaspoons dried dill

1 teaspoon mustard powder

1 teaspoon freshly squeezed lemon juice

¼ teaspoon sea salt

FOR THE WRAPS

4 whole-grain or brown rice tortillas

4 large romaine or butter lettuce leaves or arugula

2 dill pickles, sliced

1 large tomato, chopped

1 cup sprouts or microgreens

These wraps were inspired by my all-time favorite health food store, Oryana, located in Traverse City, Michigan. Though they've since renamed it, their "Hot to Trot" tofu wrap is the ultimate comfort food classic. I'd always get it with some crunchy veggies on the side and a cup of "Hummingbird Tea" made by a local organic tea farmer.

TO MAKE THE DILLY TOFU SALAD

1. Squeeze the tofu over the sink with your hands to remove excess moisture, then crumble it into a bowl.

2. Stir the carrot, Cashew Ranch Dressing, bell pepper, pickle, onion, garlic, dill, mustard, lemon juice, and salt into the tofu and mix until well combined. Set aside.

TO MAKE THE WRAPS

1. In a dry skillet, warm the tortillas over medium-high heat for up to 1 minute per side, until just heated through.

2. Top evenly with the tofu mixture, then add the lettuce, pickles, tomato, and sprouts. Enjoy immediately.

Substitution tip: If you want to make a quicker version of this salad, use a jarred vegan mayo or vegan ranch dressing instead of the Cashew Ranch Dressing.

Per serving: Calories: 235; Fat: 8g; Carbohydrates: 29g; Fiber: 5g; Protein: 11g; Sodium: 452mg; Iron: 2mg

RAW NORI ROLLS

SERVES 4

Prep Time: 10 minutes

- GLUTEN-FREE
- PLAN AHEAD

4 nori sheets

1½ cups Cashew-Macadamia Cheese (page 204)

¼ cup fermented vegetables or sauerkraut

1 small cucumber, julienned

1 scallion, both green and white parts, chopped

This is high-vibe food that will satisfy your taste buds as well as your body. Rolling nori takes a little practice, so don't despair if your first efforts turn out a bit sloppy—it'll still be delicious. For an even easier take on this dish, tear the nori into strips, place the fillings and cheese over lettuce, and make this a nori bowl. You can use the nori strips to scoop up the fillings and cheese as you go.

1. Place one sheet of nori, shiny-side down, on a clean, dry surface. Gently spread about ⅓ cup of the cheese evenly onto the lower half of the nori.

2. Distribute the fermented vegetables, cucumber, and scallion evenly across the middle of the cheese in a straight horizontal line.

3. Using both of your hands, roll the wrap up, bringing the bottom of the nori up and over the fillings, gently squeezing in order to stabilize the fillings.

4. Roll the rest of the way up. With your finger, spread a little water along the upper, top edge of the nori to seal it.

5. Place the nori roll seam-side down on a cutting board. Wet a sharp knife with water and cut the nori roll into slices. Continue to wet the knife as often as necessary. If your knife remains wet and free of debris, your nori roll pieces will be much neater and less likely to tear.

6. Repeat with the remaining nori, spread, and fillings, and serve immediately.

Variation tip: This will work with any variety of fillings. Try it with the Edamame Miso Hummus (page 66) or other vegetables in the filling.

Per serving: Calories: 266; Fat: 20g; Carbohydrates: 15g; Fiber: 6g; Protein: 11g; Sodium: 103mg; Iron: 3mg

SUPERFOOD SAMMIES

SERVES 4

Prep Time: 5 minutes

◔ PLAN AHEAD

8 whole-grain or gluten-free bread slices

½ cup Cashew-Macadamia Cheese
(page 204)

1 avocado, peeled, pitted, and sliced

½ cup onion or chive microgreens or thinly
sliced red onion

½ cup fermented vegetables, sauerkraut,
or pickles

1 tomato, sliced

1 cup baby spinach or kale

Put on your cape and prepare for greatness. This sandwich has it all—omega-rich fats to give your brain a boost, exponentially nutritious microgreens, dark leafy greens, and digestive-boosting fermented veggies. We like to buy microgreens at our local farmers' market, but I've seen them popping up everywhere (even traditional grocery stores). Microgreens are one of the most nutrient-dense foods on the planet, and super tasty to boot. We love arugula, basil, and kale microgreens, but the onion or chive ones are a great way to get that oniony flavor that's perfect here.

1. Place the bread on plates and spread the cheese evenly on 4 slices of bread. Divide the avocado slices evenly between the remaining 4 slices of bread.

2. Evenly distribute the microgreens, fermented vegetables, tomato, and spinach over the avocado sides of the sandwiches. Top with the cheese-covered slice of bread, cut in half, and enjoy immediately.

———————————

Make it WFPB: Omit the salt from the Cashew-Macadamia Cheese.

Per serving: Calories: 395; Fat: 18g; Carbohydrates: 49g;
Fiber: 15g; Protein: 15g; Sodium: 496mg; Iron: 5mg

GARDEN COLLARD WRAPS

SERVES 4

Prep Time: 20 minutes

- GLUTEN-FREE
- LEFTOVER-FRIENDLY
- PLAN AHEAD

4 large collard green leaves

1 cup Cashew-Macadamia Cheese (page 204)

1 large tomato, chopped

½ cup grated carrot

½ cup minced red bell pepper

½ cup diced cucumber

⅓ cup minced red onion

There's something so joyful about a stuffed collard wrap—the creamy vegan cheese, the rainbow of nutrient-dense vegetables, the plant-strong wrapping. What's not to love? You can play with different fillings here. The Edamame Miso Hummus (page 66) is also delicious in place of the Cashew-Macadamia Cheese for a change of pace. Or, use the Pizza Hummus (page 72) in place of or in addition to the Cashew-Macadamia Cheese and fill with tomato, kalamata olives, spinach, basil, toasted pine nuts, and some Plantstrong Parm (page 200) for a "pizza wrap."

1. Place a collard leaf stem-side up on a plate. Using a sharp knife, shave off most of the stem so that it's flush with the leaf. If you accidentally cut into the leaf, don't worry—you can roll that part up. You're aiming for an even, flat surface with no thick stem sticking up. Repeat with remaining collard greens.

2. With the stem sides facing you, spread the middle of each leaf with one-quarter of the cheese and top with tomato. Evenly add the carrot, bell pepper, cucumber, and onion. Roll the bottom of the collard leaf up and over the fillings. Roll the sides in toward the center, so that they're parallel to each other. Then, roll the wrap all the way up to form a green "burrito."

3. Repeat with the remaining ingredients and enjoy. If you have leftover wraps, they will keep, refrigerated in an airtight container, for up to 2 days.

Make it WFPB: Omit the salt from the Cashew-Macadamia Cheese.

Per serving: Calories: 192; Fat: 13g; Carbohydrates: 13g; Fiber: 4g; Protein: 8g; Sodium: 24mg; Iron: 2mg

LETTUCE WRAP TACOS

SERVES 4

Prep Time: 5 minutes

- GLUTEN-FREE
- LEFTOVER-FRIENDLY
- PLAN AHEAD

8 large leaves romaine lettuce

Cauliflower Taco Meat (page 213)

2 cups Low-Fat Cheese Dip (page 208)

2 large tomatoes, chopped

½ cup minced fresh cilantro

2 scallions, both green and white parts, minced

These tasty "tacos" couldn't be simpler, healthier, or yummier. For an alternative filling option, you can use the Walnut-Quinoa Crumbles (page 124) instead of the Cauliflower Taco Meat—either will be unbearably delicious. Serve these crunchy lettuce wrap tacos along with some Tempeh Corn Chili (page 106) for a perfectly balanced, satisfying meal.

To make the "tacos," simply fill each romaine leaf evenly with the Cauliflower Taco Meat and top with the Low-Fat Cheese Dip. Sprinkle the tomatoes, cilantro, and scallions over the top and enjoy immediately.

Substitution tip: Omit the tomatoes, scallions, and cilantro and instead use the Classic Salsa (page 202), or prepared salsa of your choice. You can also substitute Classic Guacamole (page 64) for the cheese dip if you like.

Meal prep it: You can make the Cauliflower Taco Meat ahead of time (or even a double batch of it) so that it's easy to reheat when you want to make these wraps. You can also keep the Low-Fat Cheese Dip on hand and keep your scallions minced in the refrigerator (stored in an airtight container for up to 5 days).

Per serving: Calories: 240; Fat: 8g; Carbohydrates: 31g; Fiber: 10g; Protein: 14g; Sodium: 478mg; Iron: 4mg

WALNUT-QUINOA CHIPOTLE BURRITOS

SERVES 6 TO 8

Prep Time: 20 minutes, plus overnight soaking

Cook Time: 15 minutes

○ GLUTEN-FREE
○ PLAN AHEAD

FOR THE WALNUT-QUINOA CRUMBLES

½ cup quinoa

1 cup raw walnuts

3 large garlic cloves, peeled

2 teaspoons salt-free chili powder

2 teaspoons onion granules or powder

1 teaspoon ground cumin

1 teaspoon dried oregano

½ teaspoon dried chipotle powder

½ teaspoon sea salt

FOR THE BURRITOS

6 to 8 whole-grain or brown rice tortillas

1 cup Low-Fat Cheese Dip (page 208) or Classic Guacamole (page 64)

½ cup Chipotle Cream Sauce (page 206)

4 cups raw vegetables of choice

Fun fact: You may be wondering why I call for soaked quinoa. While it's not a necessity, I like to cook ingredients as little as possible to preserve the maximum amount of nutrients. If you prefer, you can omit the quinoa and substitute 1 cup additional walnuts or cooked quinoa.

Per serving: Calories: 288; Fat: 15g; Carbohydrates: 34g; Fiber: 6g; Protein: 9g; Sodium: 63mg; Iron: 2mg

I love these burritos because they're bursting with both nutrients and flavor. The Walnut-Quinoa Crumbles are also scrumptious in tacos, on salads, or in any other Mexican dish where you might find ground meat. I personally use the dehydrator method noted below, but they're delicious either way.

TO MAKE THE WALNUT-QUINOA CRUMBLES

1. In a small bowl, cover the quinoa in plenty of water and soak for 6 to 8 hours. Drain and rinse.

2. Preheat the oven to 300°F. Line two baking sheets with silicone mats or aluminum foil.

3. In a food processor, combine the drained quinoa with the walnuts, garlic, chili powder, onion granules, cumin, oregano, chipotle, and salt. Pulse until well combined, but not entirely smooth.

4. Spread the mixture out on the baking sheets and bake for 15 minutes, or until lightly browned and crisp. Set aside.

TO MAKE THE BURRITOS

1. In a dry skillet, warm the tortillas over medium-high heat for up to 1 minute per side, until just heated through.

2. To serve, place about ⅓ cup of the Walnut-Quinoa Crumbles in each tortilla, top with Low-Fat Cheese Dip and Chipotle Cream Sauce, and then add the vegetables of your choice (I use shredded lettuce, grated carrots, and chopped red cabbage). Roll up and enjoy immediately.

Variation tip: For a totally "raw" version, place the Walnut-Quinoa Crumbles mix on dehydrator sheets for about 4 hours at 105°F, or until dry and crumbly. Then serve in lettuce or cabbage leaves with Chipotle Cream Sauce or Classic Guacamole and the raw vegetables. Delicious and so very vibrant.

MASHED POTATO JALAPEÑO BURRITOS

SERVES 6

Prep Time: 30 minutes
Cook Time: 22 minutes

- GLUTEN-FREE
- PLAN AHEAD

1 (15-ounce) can pinto beans, drained and rinsed, or 1½ cups cooked pinto beans (see page 17)

6 whole-grain or brown rice tortillas

2½ cups Garlic Mashed Potatoes (page 68)

1 to 2 jalapeños, seeded and thinly sliced

1 large carrot, grated

1 cup finely chopped purple or green cabbage

2 scallions, both green and white parts, minced

¾ cup Avotillo Sauce (page 201), Low-Fat Cheese Dip (page 208), or Classic Salsa (page 202)

These burritos are the perfect way to use up leftover mashed potatoes. You can vary the vegetables as you like and play with sauce combinations. When we're feeling "extra," we grill up onions and zucchini as another filling option. I suggest serving these buffet style, so that each family member can make their own burrito as they like. Jalapeño is such a great flavor and texture when paired with those creamy, luscious mashed potatoes, but of course, adjust the amount to suit your heat preference.

1. In a small pot, heat the pinto beans over low heat for 5 to 10 minutes, or until heated through. Set aside.

2. In a dry skillet, warm the tortillas over medium-high heat for up to 1 minute per side, until just heated through.

3. Place the tortillas on plates and fill evenly with the potatoes, beans, jalapeños, carrot, cabbage, and scallions. Pour the Avotillo Sauce on top and enjoy immediately.

Make it WFPB: Omit the salt from the mashed potatoes and sauce.

Per serving: Calories: 156; Fat: 2g; Carbohydrates: 30g; Fiber: 6g; Protein: 7g; Sodium: 140mg; Iron: 1mg

WEEKNIGHT TOSTADAS

MAKES 6 TOSTADAS

Prep Time: 10 minutes
Cook Time: 10 minutes

- ● GLUTEN-FREE
- ○ NUT-FREE
- ● PLAN AHEAD

6 corn tortillas (preferably sprouted)

1 (15-ounce) can fat-free refried beans

1 cup chopped romaine lettuce

1 cup grated carrot and/or red cabbage

2 medium tomatoes, chopped

⅓ cup minced fresh cilantro

½ cup Classic Salsa (page 202)

½ cup Classic Guacamole (page 64)

½ cup Cheesy Sauce (page 210) or grated vegan cheese of choice

2 limes, cut into wedges

These tostadas are the perfect solution for families where not everyone has the same preferences. We serve these buffet-style, so that everyone can customize their tostada to their liking. It's great to have a dish that makes light work for the chef and pleases everyone at the same time. Feel free to customize this with other toppings if you like, or use store-bought sauces and vegan cheese in a pinch.

1. Preheat the oven to 400°F.

2. Place the tortillas on a large baking sheet and bake for 10 minutes, or until crisp and lightly browned. Remove and set aside.

3. While the tortillas are baking, assemble the rest of the meal. In a medium pot, place the beans over low heat. Stir a little water into the beans if needed to thin. Cook for 2 to 4 minutes, stirring often, until warmed through.

4. To assemble, spread the beans on each crisp tortilla and top with the lettuce, carrot, tomatoes, and cilantro, as desired. Top with Classic Salsa, Classic Guacamole, and Cheesy Sauce and serve with a lime wedge as garnish. Serve immediately.

Variation tip: We sometimes spray the tortillas with coconut or olive oil before baking in order to give them a more "fried" feel. They're still relatively low in fat, and tend to go over better with picky kids that way.

Meal prep it: If you're like us and make these often, be sure to keep your sauces on hand for ease of preparation. You can also chop the cabbage in advance and keep it in the refrigerator in an airtight container for up to a week.

Per Serving: Calories: 168; Fat: 4g; Carbohydrates: 29g; Fiber: 7g; Protein: 6g; Sodium: 398mg; Iron: 2mg

EGGPLANT "PARMESAN" WRAPS

SERVES 6

Prep Time: 15 minutes

Cook Time: About 30 minutes

● GLUTEN-FREE
○ PLAN AHEAD

FOR THE EGGPLANT

Nonstick cooking spray (olive or sunflower oil)

1 medium eggplant, cut into ¼-inch-thick rounds

3 tablespoons plain unsweetened nondairy milk

2 tablespoons tamari, shoyu, or soy sauce

1 cup chickpea flour

4 teaspoons garlic granules or powder

1 tablespoon dried basil

1 tablespoon dried oregano

½ teaspoon sea salt

FOR THE WRAPS

6 whole-grain tortillas

4 cups chopped baby spinach or arugula

2 cups vegan marinara sauce, warmed

1½ cups Cashew-Macadamia Cheese (page 204)

⅓ cup Plantstrong Parm (page 200) (optional)

Eggplant, what right do you have to be so delicious? It's borderline rude. Sure, you need some seasonings (and a proper amount of cooking) to make you shine, but still—is it really fair to all the other vegetables? I think not. These wraps, not unlike their eggplant star, are offensively delicious, but go ahead and try them anyway.

TO MAKE THE EGGPLANT

1. Preheat the oven to 400°F. Spray a large baking sheet with cooking spray or line with a silicone liner or parchment paper and set aside.

2. In a large bowl, combine the eggplant slices, milk, and tamari. Turn the pieces over to coat them as evenly as possible with the liquids. Set aside.

3. In a medium bowl, combine the chickpea flour, garlic granules, basil, oregano, and salt and stir well. Set aside.

4. Stir the eggplant slices again and transfer to a plate (stacking is fine). Do not discard the liquid.

5. Toss an eggplant round in the flour mixture. Then, dip in the liquid again. Double up on the coating by placing the eggplant again into the flour mixture, making sure that all sides are nicely breaded. Place on the prepared baking sheet. Repeat with the remaining eggplant slices, placing them on the baking sheet in a single layer (try to leave a little space in between each piece).

6. Spray the tops of the eggplant with enough oil so that you no longer see dry patches in the coating. Bake for 15 minutes. Remove and spray the tops again. Turn each piece over and spray the tops with oil, again making sure that no dry patches remain. Bake for another 15 minutes, or until nicely browned and crisp. Remove from heat.

TO MAKE THE WRAPS

1. In a dry skillet, warm the tortillas over medium-high heat for up to 1 minute per side, until just heated through.

2. Place some spinach in the center of each. Top with the warm eggplant slices, marinara sauce, and Cashew-Macadamia Cheese. Top with the Plantstrong Parm (if using) before wrapping up the tortillas. Enjoy immediately.

Make it WFPB: Simply omit the oil spray, and use an oil-free marinara sauce.

Per serving: Calories: 540; Fat: 23g; Carbohydrates: 69g; Fiber: 17g; Protein: 23g; Sodium: 1120mg; Iron: 7mg

CLEAN MACHINE CABBAGE ROLLS

MAKES 12 ROLLS

Prep Time: 10 minutes
Cook Time: 25 minutes

- ◐ GLUTEN-FREE
- ● LEFTOVER-FRIENDLY
- ○ NUT-FREE
- ◐ PLAN AHEAD

2 (14.5-ounce) cans diced tomatoes

1¼ cups water

1 cup quinoa

¼ cup Chicky Seasoning (page 198)

4 large garlic cloves, minced or pressed

¼ to ½ teaspoon freshly ground black pepper

Sea salt (optional)

1 large head cabbage (12 leaves)

1 cup Creamy Dill Dressing (page 88), for dipping (optional, but strongly recommended)

Substitution tip: You can also use collard leaves instead of cabbage.

Ingredient tip: Different heads of cabbage may behave differently when wrapping these rolls. If you've gotten an uncooperative cabbage with leaves that are difficult to pull off, cut the base off the cabbage and steam the whole thing until it's softer and has turned a darker green. This should make it easier to remove the leaves. With this option, you don't need to steam the rolls again.

Per serving (2 rolls): Calories: 665; Fat: 6g; Carbohydrates: 124g; Fiber: 18g; Protein: 32g; Sodium: 991mg; Iron: 9mg

These nutrient-dense, high fiber, fat-free rolls are perfect for keeping your body a clean machine. And, bonus, they're really tasty, too. They're great as a side or even a main dish, with or without the dipping sauce. Try them with some Red Lentil Potato Soup (page 110) or a Vegan Cobb Salad (page 91).

1. In a large pot, combine the tomatoes and their juices, water, quinoa, Chicky Seasoning, garlic, and pepper over high heat. Cover and bring to a boil. Reduce the heat to low and simmer, mostly covered, for 15 minutes, or until all of the liquid has been absorbed and the quinoa is tender. Remove from the heat and fluff with a fork to allow steam to escape. Season with salt (if using).

2. Fill a large pot with a few inches of water and place a steaming basket inside the pot. Set aside.

3. Cut the stem off the cabbage and discard the outer leaf. Gently peel off 12 cabbage leaves and set them aside.

4. On a clean flat surface, place a cabbage leaf with the inside portion facing upward. Scoop about ¼ cup of the quinoa filling onto the lower center part of the cabbage leaf. Wrap the bottom up over the filling, then fold the sides in. Roll from the bottom up to form a burrito-like wrap. Place in the steaming basket, seam side down. Repeat with remaining leaves and filling.

5. Cover and steam over medium heat for 10 minutes, or until the cabbage leaves are bright green. Serve with the Creamy Dill Dressing (if using) for dipping. Refrigerate leftovers in an airtight container for up to a week.

THE BIG HEALTHY VEGAN CRUNCHWRAP

SERVES 4

Prep Time: 15 minutes
Cook Time: 30 minutes

◯ PLAN AHEAD

4 corn tortillas (preferably sprouted)

Nonstick cooking spray (coconut or avocado oil)

4 large whole-grain tortillas

4 small whole-grain tortillas

¾ cup fat-free vegan refried beans

¾ cup Cauliflower Taco Meat (page 213)

1 cup chopped romaine lettuce

1 large tomato, chopped

4 teaspoons neutral-flavored oil (avocado, sunflower, or sesame)

1 cup Low-Fat Cheese Dip (page 208)

½ cup Chipotle Cream Sauce (page 206)

½ cup Classic Guacamole (page 64)

Make it WFPB: Omit the oil spray and oil and use a nonstick skillet. Omit the salt from the cauliflower meat and sauces.

Per serving: Calories: 609; Fat: 23g; Carbohydrates: 85g; Fiber: 16g; Protein: 26g; Sodium: 576mg; Iron: 5mg

Confession: I didn't even know what a "crunchwrap" was until I began writing this book. But when I posted on social media asking for recipe requests, this was a popular one. So, I did some research, and discovered that it was indeed possible to create a healthy vegan version of this. Yay! I hope this fulfills all of your crunchwrap hopes, dreams, and aspirations.

1. Preheat the oven to 400°F.

2. Place the corn tortillas on a baking sheet and spray both sides with oil. Bake for 10 minutes, or until crisp and lightly browned. Remove and set aside.

3. To assemble the crunchwraps, lay out the large tortillas and place a baked corn tortilla in the center of each one. Evenly spread the refried beans over the tops of the corn tortillas. Sprinkle the Cauliflower Taco Meat, lettuce, and tomato over the top of each. Place the smaller tortilla on top of the fillings and corn tortilla. Fold the larger tortilla up and over the top, creating pleats, so that the fillings and corn tortilla are enclosed.

4. In a medium skillet, heat 1 teaspoon of the oil over low heat, distributing it evenly in the pan. Carefully place the crunchwrap, pleat-side down, in the skillet. Cover with a lid and cook for 3 to 4 minutes, or until the underside is golden brown. Spray the top of the crunchwrap with oil and gently flip over, cover again, and cook the other side for another 3 to 4 minutes, or until golden brown. Remove from the heat and repeat this process with the remaining crunchwraps. Make only as many as you'll be serving immediately, as these don't stay crisp if stored. Serve topped with any or all of the Low-Fat Cheese Dip, Chipotle Cream Sauce, and Classic Guacamole.

Bean and Rice Bowl with
Mango Salsa, page 139

NOODLES AND RICE

SIMPLE STAPLE RICE

SERVES 4

Prep Time: 5 minutes

○ GLUTEN-FREE
● LEFTOVER-FRIENDLY
○ NUT-FREE
○ PLAN AHEAD

4 cups cooked long- or short-grain brown rice (see page 18)

2 tablespoons neutral-flavored oil (refined coconut, avocado, sunflower, or raw sesame)

4 teaspoons tamari, shoyu, or soy sauce

1½ tablespoons nutritional yeast

When I was visiting friends in California decades ago, they used to make this rice for dinner almost every night. There was something so comforting and satisfying about it, despite its utter simplicity, and I found myself craving it regularly once I returned home. To this day, it remains one of my favorite dinner staples—it goes wonderfully with just about anything, but I especially love it with some salad and beans on the side.

Into individual bowls, place the cooked rice and top evenly with the oil, tamari, and nutritional yeast. Serve warm or hot. Store leftovers in an airtight container for up to a week.

———————————

Variation tip: As this dish is so simple, you can have fun creating different twists on it. Here are some ideas:

- Omit the nutritional yeast and oil, and instead add Plantstrong Parm (page 200).

- Omit the oil and tamari and top with Cheesy Sauce (page 210).

- Top with:
  - Arugula or basil microgreens
  - Your favorite fermented vegetables or sauerkraut
  - Everything Tofu (page 212)
  - Warm pinto beans and some Eat-It-Every-Day Gravy (page 211)

Make it WFPB: Omit the oil (no need to replace it with anything).

Per serving: Calories: 309; Fat: 9g; Carbohydrates: 51g; Fiber: 4g; Protein: 7g; Sodium: 731mg; Iron: 1mg

CILANTRO-LIME RICE

SERVES 4

Prep Time: 5 to 10 minutes

- ◐ GLUTEN-FREE
- ● LEFTOVER-FRIENDLY
- ○ NUT-FREE
- ◐ PLAN AHEAD

3 cups cooked short- or long-grain brown rice (see page 18)

¼ cup packed chopped fresh cilantro

3 tablespoons minced red onion

2½ tablespoons freshly squeezed lime juice

2 medium garlic cloves, minced or pressed

1 tablespoon sunflower or olive oil

½ teaspoon sea salt

We eat Mexican food on an almost daily basis in our house, and this rice gives everything an extra-special touch. Tuck it into burritos alongside black or pinto beans and some Classic Guacamole (page 64) or Avotillo Sauce (page 201). It's also satisfying in tacos, tostadas, and taco salads. For a delicious burrito bowl, top some romaine lettuce with this rice and add some refried beans, Classic Salsa (page 202), guacamole, and sautéed vegetables. Yum!

In a large bowl, mix the rice, cilantro, onion, lime juice, garlic, oil, and salt. Stir well. Serve warm or cold. Refrigerate in an airtight container for up to 5 days.

_____

Make it WFPB: Omit the oil and add a little extra water as needed for moisture.

Variation tip: For a complete yet simple meal, you can substitute 1 cup of black or pinto beans for 1 cup of the rice. Season the same and serve warm or cold.

Per serving: Calories: 546; Fat: 7g; Carbohydrates: 104g; Fiber: 6g; Protein: 9g; Sodium: 1mg; Iron: 3mg

INDIAN-SPICED LEMON RICE

SERVES 3 TO 5

Prep Time: 5 minutes
Cook Time: 6 to 8 minutes

● GLUTEN-FREE
● LEFTOVER-FRIENDLY
○ NUT-FREE
● PLAN AHEAD

1 tablespoon sunflower or coconut oil

1 tablespoon brown mustard seeds

1 teaspoon cumin seeds

⅓ cup minced white or yellow onion

½ teaspoon asafetida

¼ teaspoon ground turmeric

3 cups cooked short-grain brown rice (see page 18), cooled

2 tablespoons freshly squeezed lemon juice

2 large garlic cloves, minced or pressed

½ teaspoon sea salt

Asafetida is a traditional Indian seasoning that I fell in love with at first taste about 25 years ago. It's available in international grocery stores or Indian markets—however, if you can't find it, just add an extra clove or two of garlic. This delicious, delicately spiced dish is great alongside some Red Lentil Dal (page 108) or the Chickpea Potato Curry (page 165).

1. In a large skillet or wok, combine the oil, mustard seeds, and cumin seeds over medium-high heat. Stir-fry for about a minute, or until the seeds begin to pop.

2. Add the onion, asafetida, and turmeric. Cook for 3 to 5 minutes, stirring often, until the onion begins to brown.

3. Add the rice, lemon juice, garlic, and salt. Cook another 1 to 2 minutes, stirring constantly, until thoroughly combined and warmed all the way through. Serve immediately. Refrigerate leftovers in an airtight container for up to a week.

Make it WFPB: Omit the oil and sauté the mustard seeds, cumin seeds, turmeric, asafetida (if using), and onion in about 2 tablespoons water, until the onion is softened, about 3 minutes. Then, add the garlic, lemon juice, salt, and rice. Cook for another 2 minutes or so, until warmed through. If the mixture gets dry during cooking, add a little more water as you go.

Per serving: Calories: 456; Fat: 6g; Carbohydrates: 84g; Fiber: 5g; Protein: 7g; Sodium: 1mg; Iron: 3mg

CAULIFLOWER FRIED "RICE"

SERVES 3 TO 5

Prep Time: 5 minutes
Cook Time: 10 minutes

- ○ 30 MINUTES OR LESS
- ● GLUTEN-FREE
- ○ NUT-FREE

4 cups packed riced cauliflower or 1 (12-ounce) bag frozen cauliflower rice, thawed

2 cups sliced shiitake mushroom caps

⅓ cup diced carrot

½ to 1 cup water, divided

⅔ cup corn kernels

2 scallions, both white and green parts, minced (about ⅔ cup)

⅓ cup peas

2 tablespoons coconut aminos, shoyu, tamari, or soy sauce

4 large garlic cloves, minced or pressed

1 tablespoon toasted sesame oil

Sriracha sauce or chili garlic sauce, for serving (optional)

This is a dish I make for myself all the time—I love how it makes me feel like I'm eating a huge bowl of food, yet it's very light (almost entirely vegetables), nutritious, and satisfying. I especially like to enjoy this with a few Fresh Spring Rolls with Peanut Sauce (page 77) on the side. You can also top this "rice" with some Everything Tofu (page 212) to make it extra fabulous.

1. In a large wok or skillet, combine the cauliflower, mushrooms, carrot, and ¼ cup of water over medium-high heat. Cook for about 5 minutes, stirring often, until the water is absorbed and the cauliflower is just tender. If necessary, add up to ¼ cup additional water to prevent sticking.

2. Add the corn, scallions, peas, ¼ cup water, coconut aminos, garlic, and oil. Cook, stirring frequently, for another 5 minutes, or until all of the water is absorbed and the vegetables are tender but still slightly crisp. If necessary, add up to ¼ cup additional water to prevent sticking. Serve immediately, topped with sriracha (if using).

Make it WFPB: Replace the sesame oil with additional water.

Per serving: Calories: 108; Fat: 4g; Carbohydrates: 15g; Fiber: 5g; Protein: 6g; Sodium: 607mg; Iron: 1mg

BROWN RICE AND VEGGIE BOWL WITH GRAVY

SERVES 4

Prep Time: 10 minutes
Cook Time: 20 minutes

- ● GLUTEN-FREE
- ● LEFTOVER-FRIENDLY
- ● PLAN AHEAD

2 cups diced zucchini

2 cups diced red bell pepper

8 cups baby spinach

4 cups cooked brown rice (see page 18)

2 cups grated carrots

2 cups Eat-It-Every-Day Gravy (page 211)

Everything Tofu (page 212) (optional)

This is one of those dishes that our family loves to keep on regular rotation because it's healthy, delicious, and so very versatile. We often set it up like a buffet, with lots of different options so that everyone can customize their own bowl. One thing I especially love is that this combines both cooked and raw foods so you can have the best of both worlds.

1. Preheat the oven to 400°F.

2. On a nonstick or silicone-lined baking sheet, spread the zucchini and bell pepper in a single layer and bake for 10 minutes. Remove, toss, and bake for another 10 minutes, or until lightly browned and tender.

3. Into individual bowls, divide the spinach and top with the warm or hot rice. Layer on the roasted zucchini-pepper mixture and grated carrots. Pour a generous amount of Eat-It-Every-Day Gravy over the top and sprinkle with Everything Tofu (if using). Enjoy immediately.

Meal prep it: To make this an extra-easy weeknight staple, keep cooked rice and the gravy on hand. You can also pre-roast the zucchini-pepper mixture. Keep those three items in airtight containers in the refrigerator and gently reheat them when you're ready to make your bowls. Dinner will be ready in under 10 minutes.

Per serving: Calories: 494; Fat: 9g; Carbohydrates: 85g; Fiber: 16g; Protein: 21g; Sodium: 894mg; Iron: 6mg

BEAN AND RICE BOWL WITH MANGO SALSA

SERVES 4

Prep Time: 10 minutes
Cook Time: 5 minutes

- ● GLUTEN-FREE
- ○ NUT-FREE
- ● PLAN AHEAD

FOR THE SALSA

4 cups diced mango

½ cup minced red onion

½ cup chopped fresh cilantro

¼ cup freshly squeezed lime juice

¾ teaspoon sea salt

¼ to ¾ teaspoon red pepper flakes

FOR THE RICE BOWL

1 (15-ounce) can black beans, drained and rinsed, or 1½ cups cooked black beans (see page 17)

4 cups chopped butter or romaine lettuce

4 cups cooked brown rice (see page 18)

1½ cups grated carrots or chopped red cabbage

½ cup thinly sliced scallions

This simple bowl, topped with a mouthwatering bright mango salsa that really makes it shine, is a perfect weeknight meal that can be thrown together in minutes. Feel free to vary the vegetables you're using, and even add in some roasted vegetables, such as onions and zucchini. We especially love this with the Classic Guacamole (page 64) on top.

TO MAKE THE SALSA

In a small bowl, combine the mango, onion, cilantro, lime juice, salt, and red pepper flakes and stir well. Set aside.

TO MAKE THE RICE BOWLS

1. In a small pot, warm the beans over low heat, stirring often, for 2 to 3 minutes, or until hot. Remove from heat.

2. Into individual bowls, divide the lettuce evenly. Top with the rice, beans, and carrots. Evenly top with the salsa, and garnish with scallions. Enjoy immediately.

Make it WFPB: Omit the salt.

Per serving: Calories: 459; Fat: 2g; Carbohydrates: 97g; Fiber: 14g; Protein: 13g; Sodium: 434mg; Iron: 7mg

BAJA BOWL WITH AVOTILLO SAUCE

SERVES 4

Prep Time: 10 minutes
Cook Time: 20 minutes

○ 30 MINUTES OR LESS
● GLUTEN-FREE
○ NUT-FREE

2 teaspoons olive oil

1 large red onion, thinly sliced

1 orange bell pepper, chopped or sliced into strips

1 (15-ounce) can pinto beans, drained and rinsed, or 1½ cups cooked pinto beans (see page 17)

8 cups baby greens

4 cups cooked quinoa (see page 18)

2 cups Avotillo Sauce (page 201)

½ cup chopped fresh cilantro, for garnish

¼ cup roasted pumpkin seeds or pepitas, for garnish

Although this isn't technically a noodle or rice dish, I snuck it into this chapter because quinoa can be a great alternative to rice. This dish is so brightly colored and flavorful that you may forget it's actually good for you. I love all-in-one dishes like this that supply your veggies along with your entrée. Feel free to vary the vegetables (broccoli and other types of bell peppers are great in this), as well as the type of bean (try black beans or black-eyed peas).

1. In a large skillet, heat the oil over medium-high heat. Cook the onion and pepper for 5 to 10 minutes, stirring often, until the onion begins to brown. Remove from heat.

2. In a small pot, warm the beans over low heat, stirring often, for 1 to 2 minutes. Set aside.

3. In individual bowls, place the baby greens and top evenly with the quinoa, onion-pepper mixture, and beans. Pour the Avotillo Sauce over the top and garnish with cilantro and pumpkin seeds. Serve immediately.

Make it WFPB: Stir-fry the onion and pepper in water instead of oil and omit the salt from the Avotillo Sauce.

Per serving: Calories: 910; Fat: 20g; Carbohydrates: 144g; Fiber: 22g; Protein: 34g; Sodium: 120mg; Iron: 7mg

SMOKY BEANS, RICE, AND KALE

SERVES 4

Prep Time: 5 minutes
Cook Time: 45 minutes

● GLUTEN-FREE
● LEFTOVER-FRIENDLY
○ NUT-FREE
● PLAN AHEAD

2 cups water

1 cup long-grain brown rice

¼ cup Chicky Seasoning (page 198)

4 large garlic cloves, pressed or minced

1 cup lightly packed kale, stemmed and cut into thin ribbons

1 (15-ounce) can black or red beans, rinsed and drained, or 1½ cups cooked black beans (see page 17)

2 tablespoons extra-virgin olive oil

1 teaspoon liquid smoke

½ teaspoon sea salt

I was inspired to create this dish after inviting friends over for Thanksgiving one year. They made some of the best beans and rice I'd ever had, and I was determined to replicate it. This hearty dish is so satisfying, you can easily make it into a meal on its own. However, it's also great paired with a tangy salad such as the Kuchumber (page 84), Romaine Salad with Magical Ginger Dressing (page 95), or Cauliflower Tabbouleh (page 87).

1. In a medium pot, combine the water, rice, Chicky Seasoning, and garlic. Bring to a boil, then reduce to a simmer for 45 minutes, or until the rice is tender and the water is fully absorbed.

2. As soon as the rice is done, stir in the kale so that it wilts from the heat. Add the beans, oil, liquid smoke, and salt. Stir very well and serve immediately. Refrigerate leftovers in an airtight container for up to a week.

Make it WFPB: Omit the olive oil and sea salt.

Per serving: Calories: 474; Fat: 8g; Carbohydrates: 86g; Fiber: 11g; Protein: 12g; Sodium: 9mg; Iron: 4mg

PAD THAI

SERVES 4

Prep Time: 10 to 15 minutes
Cook Time: Up to 10 minutes

○ 30 MINUTES OR LESS
◐ GLUTEN-FREE
● LEFTOVER-FRIENDLY

8 ounces brown rice pad thai noodles

3 scallions, both green and white parts, minced

⅓ cup chopped fresh cilantro

¼ cup maple syrup

3 tablespoons freshly squeezed lime juice

2 tablespoons tamari, shoyu, or soy sauce

2 tablespoons neutral-flavored oil (sunflower, raw sesame, or avocado)

1½ tablespoons ketchup

1 tablespoon hot sauce (cayenne or tabasco)

3 large garlic cloves, pressed or minced

½ teaspoon plus ⅛ teaspoon sea salt

1 cup bean sprouts

¼ cup crushed peanuts

This pad thai is easy and mouthwateringly tasty, and can be made with ingredients found in any supermarket. For an impressive feast, serve with Fresh Spring Rolls with Peanut Sauce (page 77), and garnish the noodles with lime wedges for added zing. When I serve these noodles to guests, there are never any leftovers—so if you want to avoid a tragedy, I suggest making a double batch.

1. Bring a large pot of water to a boil and prepare the noodles according to the package instructions. Once al dente, drain and set aside.

2. While the noodles are cooking, in a large bowl, combine the scallions, cilantro, maple syrup, lime juice, tamari, oil, ketchup, hot sauce, and garlic and stir well.

3. Stir the noodles into the sauce and gently toss until the noodles are coated.

4. Serve topped with the bean sprouts and peanuts. Refrigerate leftovers (if you're lucky enough to have any) in an airtight container for up to 3 days.

Variation tip: If you've got some extra bok choy on hand, that goes very nicely in this pad thai, too (pictured). Sauté it with some thinly sliced shallots before adding both to the bowl of noodles and sauce.

Make it WFPB: Omit the oil and salt, and substitute 1 tablespoon peanut butter that's been whisked with 1 tablespoon water. It will have less of an authentic pad thai flavor this way, but will still be totally delicious.

Per serving: Calories: 390; Fat: 12g; Carbohydrates: 65g; Fiber: 4g; Protein: 8g; Sodium: 582mg; Iron: 2mg

ZOODLES AND NOODLES

SERVES 4

Prep Time: 5 minutes
Cook Time: 10 minutes

○ 30 MINUTES OR LESS
◐ GLUTEN-FREE
● LEFTOVER-FRIENDLY

8 ounces brown rice spaghetti or capellini (I use Jovial brand)

4 cups frozen or fresh zucchini noodles

4 cups vegan marinara sauce of choice

½ cup Plantstrong Parm (page 200) or ½ cup Cashew-Macadamia Cheese (page 204) (optional)

¼ cup thinly sliced fresh basil

I always see recipes that have either zucchini noodles or regular pasta. In my opinion, an all-zucchini noodle option is a little unsatisfying, but an all-pasta option can feel a bit heavy. Hence, my solution—the half and half. This super simple recipe combines zoodles *and* noodles, so you can eat a big plate of pasta without all the calories. A total win! You can use this concept for any kind of pasta, so feel free to get creative. Make this with Cheesy Sauce (page 210) instead of marinara, or opt for Peanut Sauce (page 207) for an Asian-style flair.

1. Bring a large pot of water to boil and add the pasta noodles.

2. After about 5 minutes, add the zucchini noodles if using frozen. If using fresh, wait until the pasta is almost done.

3. Cook until the pasta is al dente and the zucchini is bright green. Drain and serve topped with the marinara sauce and a sprinkle of cheese (if using). Garnish with fresh basil. Refrigerate leftovers in an airtight container for up to 3 days.

Ingredient tip: We often opt for the easy route and buy organic frozen zucchini noodles at Costco. However, with an inexpensive vegetable spiralizer, you can easily make them at home. I recommend the Veggetti brand, as it's only around $10 and works very well.

Per serving: Calories: 282; Fat: 2g; Carbohydrates: 59g; Fiber: 7g; Protein: 9g; Sodium: 1127mg; Iron: 1mg

CHILI-LIME NOODLES

SERVES 4

Prep Time: 10 minutes

Cook Time: 10 minutes

○ 30 MINUTES OR LESS
◑ GLUTEN-FREE
● LEFTOVER-FRIENDLY
○ NUT-FREE
○ WFPB

8 ounces brown rice noodles

½ cup freshly squeezed lime juice

¼ cup tamari, shoyu, or soy sauce

¼ cup maple syrup

3 tablespoons finely grated fresh ginger

4 large garlic cloves, minced or pressed

2 tablespoons sriracha sauce

1 cup chopped fresh cilantro

1 cup diced cucumber

2 large scallions, both green and white parts, chopped (about ⅔ cup)

This dish has it all. It's absolutely scrumptious, easy to make, and so nutrient-dense that I use it as a way to boost my immune system when I'm feeling under the weather. I've been making variations of this dish for the last 10 years, but this version is my favorite because of how light yet full-flavored it is. Serve this on weeknights (the whole dish comes together while the noodles are cooking) or for special occasions, topped with crushed peanuts and with Fresh Spring Rolls with Peanut Sauce (page 77) on the side.

1. Bring a large pot of water to a boil and cook the noodles according to the package directions. Once al dente, drain.

2. While the noodles are cooking, in a large bowl, combine the lime juice, tamari, maple syrup, ginger, garlic, and sriracha. Whisk well. Add the cilantro, cucumber, and scallions. Once the noodles are ready, add them to the bowl and toss gently, just enough to coat them with the sauce and vegetables, and serve. Refrigerate leftovers in an airtight container for up to 3 days. I recommend eating them cold as leftovers, as they lose some freshness if reheated.

Variation tip: For a richer dish, add a tablespoon of toasted sesame oil to the sauce and/or top with ¼ cup chopped, dry-roasted peanuts.

Per serving: Calories: 339; Fat: 6g; Carbohydrates: 64g; Fiber: 3g; Protein: 7g; Sodium: 1084mg; Iron: 2mg

IMMUNE-BOOSTING LIME-GINGER-MISO NOODLES

SERVES 4

Prep Time: 10 minutes

Cook Time: About 10 minutes

○ 30 MINUTES OR LESS
◐ GLUTEN-FREE
● LEFTOVER-FRIENDLY
○ NUT-FREE

8 ounces brown rice noodles

2 tablespoons plus 1 teaspoon tamari, shoyu, or soy sauce, divided

4 large garlic cloves, minced or pressed

1 tablespoon grated ginger

1 tablespoon miso (any variety)

1 tablespoon toasted sesame oil

1 tablespoon freshly squeezed lime juice

2 cups sliced shiitake mushrooms

5 scallions, both green and white parts, cut into 1-inch pieces

These noodles may be ridiculously good for you (thanks to immune-boosting ginger, miso, lime, garlic, and shiitakes), but they're also absolutely scrumptious! You can serve these plain or topped with Everything Tofu (page 212) and a sprinkling of toasted sesame seeds. This dish makes for a healthy feast when served with Fresh Spring Rolls with Peanut Sauce (page 77) and/or Toasted Sesame Sushi with Ginger-Lime Sauce (page 116).

1. Bring a large pot of water to a boil and cook the noodles according to package instructions (I use Jovial brand capellini or spaghetti). Once al dente, drain and set aside.

2. While the noodles are cooking, in a large bowl, place 2 tablespoons tamari, garlic, ginger, miso, oil, and lime juice. Whisk or stir and set aside.

3. In a medium skillet or wok, stir-fry the mushrooms in the remaining 1 teaspoon tamari (adding a little water as needed) for 3 to 5 minutes, or until soft. Add the scallions and cook for another minute. Remove from heat.

4. Add the noodles to the sauce bowl and toss gently until coated with the sauce. Add the veggies and lightly stir. Serve hot or warm. Refrigerate leftovers in an airtight container for up to a week.

Make it WFPB: Omit the oil and top the noodles with ¼ cup toasted sesame seeds.

Per serving: Calories: 262; Fat: 5g; Carbohydrates: 49g; Fiber: 3g; Protein: 6g; Sodium: 433mg; Iron: 2mg

GREEN CURRY NOODLES

SERVES 6 TO 8

Prep Time: 10 minutes
Cook Time: 10 minutes

○ 30 MINUTES OR LESS
◐ GLUTEN-FREE
● LEFTOVER-FRIENDLY
○ NUT-FREE

8 ounces brown rice pad thai noodles

1 (13.5-ounce) can full-fat coconut milk, divided

¼ cup green curry paste

¼ cup freshly squeezed lime juice

3 tablespoons grated fresh ginger

4 large garlic cloves, minced or pressed

1 teaspoon sea salt

1 cup thinly sliced fresh basil, divided

½ cup chopped fresh cilantro

1 large carrot, grated

3 scallions, both green and white parts, minced

These yummy, easy-to-make noodles will be a hit at your next party, family dinner, or potluck. They can either be served plain or topped with Everything Tofu (page 212) or crushed peanuts. If possible, serve them soon after making them, as they tend to thicken a bit once refrigerated.

1. Bring a large pot of water to a boil and prepare the noodles according to the package instructions. Once al dente, drain.

2. Meanwhile, in a very large bowl, add about ¼ cup of the coconut milk and green curry paste (I use Thai Kitchen brand). Whisk well until smooth. Add the remaining coconut milk, lime juice, ginger, garlic, and salt. Whisk well.

3. Add half of the basil to the bowl, along with the cilantro, carrot, and scallions. Stir well.

4. When the noodles are ready, add them to the bowl. Gently toss until the noodles are coated evenly with the sauce. Serve warm, topped with the remaining basil. If you have leftovers, refrigerate them in an airtight container for up to 3 days, although they will thicken considerably.

Ingredient tip: Curry paste tends to vary in heat levels. At ¼ cup, the brand I used (Thai Kitchen) didn't produce an overly spicy result, but some brands may. If you're unable to find the Thai Kitchen brand, you may want to begin with 2 to 3 tablespoons of curry paste and increase as desired.

Per serving: Calories: 214; Fat: 10g; Carbohydrates: 27g; Fiber: 2g; Protein: 3g; Sodium: 267mg; Iron: 1mg

STUFFED SHELLS

SERVES 3 TO 4

Prep Time: 10 minutes
Cook Time: 30 minutes

- GLUTEN-FREE
- LEFTOVER-FRIENDLY
- PLAN AHEAD

8 ounces whole-grain or gluten-free large pasta shells

2 cups crumbled firm or extra-firm tofu

1 tablespoon extra-virgin olive oil

2 cups loosely packed spinach

2 tablespoons nutritional yeast

2 tablespoons freshly squeezed lemon juice

4 large garlic cloves, minced or pressed

1 teaspoon onion granules or powder

¾ teaspoon sea salt

Freshly ground black pepper

1½ cups vegan pasta sauce of choice

¾ cup Cashew-Macadamia Cheese (page 204) or shredded vegan cheese of choice

A really cool thing about pasta these days is that you can find such a huge variety of healthy, high-fiber options. One of my favorites is the green lentil lasagna noodles by Explore Cuisine, which I often use in this dish when I want to take the lazy route and swap noodles for shells. To do this, simply layer the noodles with the filling, sauce, and cheese. Easy peasy!

1. Preheat the oven to 425°F.

2. Bring a large pot of water to a boil. Cook the shells according to the package instructions, until a little firmer than al dente, 10 to 12 minutes (they'll get softer after you put the completed dish into the oven). Drain immediately and rinse under cold water. Drain again.

3. While the noodles are cooking, using your hands, squeeze the excess water from the tofu. In a large pan or wok, heat the oil over medium-high heat and sauté the tofu and spinach for a minute, then add the nutritional yeast, lemon juice, garlic, onion granules, salt, and pepper. Stir well and cook until the spinach is lightly wilted. Remove from heat.

4. In a large baking dish, spread ½ cup of pasta sauce in a thin layer on the bottom. Fill each shell with about 2 tablespoons of the tofu-spinach filling and place in the dish on top of the sauce. (If using lasagna noodles, just place them in the pan in a single layer on top of the sauce, then top them with the tofu mixture). Continue this until the pasta and filling are both used up.

CONTINUED ▶

5. Top the shells evenly with more pasta sauce (about a cup), spreading it around evenly with the back of a spoon. Sprinkle or spoon the cheese over the top.

6. Bake for 10 minutes, then set the oven to broil. Cook the pasta under the broiler until the cheese is bubbly and the noodles are browned on the edges, about 5 minutes. Remove from oven and enjoy. Refrigerate leftovers in an airtight container for up to 5 days.

Make it WFPB: Use water instead of oil to sauté the spinach-tofu mixture. For an even lower-fat version, use Low-Fat Cheese Dip (page 208) instead of the Cashew-Macadamia Cheese.

Per serving: Calories: 420; Fat: 13g; Carbohydrates: 60g; Fiber: 4g; Protein: 17g; Sodium: 2444mg; Iron: 4mg

ASIAN-INSPIRED CREAMY KELP NOODLES

SERVES 4

Prep Time: 20 minutes, plus noodle soaking time

- GLUTEN-FREE
- LEFTOVER-FRIENDLY
- PLAN AHEAD
- WFPB

FOR THE SAUCE

¼ cup unsalted raw cashew pieces, soaked, drained, and rinsed (see page 11)

¼ cup peanut butter powder

¼ cup water

3 tablespoons tamari, shoyu, or soy sauce

3 large garlic cloves, peeled

1-inch fresh ginger piece

Zest and juice of 1 large lime (2 tablespoons juice)

2 tablespoons coconut sugar

1 tablespoon toasted sesame seeds (see Ingredient tip, page 83)

⅛ teaspoon ground cayenne

FOR THE NOODLES

1 (12-ounce) bag kelp noodles

1 tablespoon apple cider vinegar

1 cup finely chopped purple cabbage

1 medium carrot, grated or julienned

2 scallions, both green and white parts, chopped

¼ cup chopped fresh cilantro

Kelp noodles are extremely low in calories and a great source of minerals. They're also really different than any other type of noodle, in that they take some coaxing before they're ready to eat. Mainly, they need to be tenderized and paired with a creamy sauce (like the one here). Kelp noodles are also great paired with steamed broccoli and Cheesy Sauce (page 210). Enjoy!

TO MAKE THE SAUCE

In a blender, combine the cashews, peanut butter powder, water, tamari, garlic, ginger, lime zest and juice, coconut sugar, sesame seeds, and cayenne. Blend until completely smooth. If necessary, add up to 2 tablespoons additional water. Pour the sauce over the vegetables.

TO MAKE THE NOODLES

1. Drain the kelp noodles and place in a bowl. Cover with water and stir in the vinegar. Allow to sit for an hour or longer.

2. While the noodles are soaking, in a large bowl, combine the cabbage, carrot, scallions, and cilantro. Set aside.

3. Drain and rinse the noodles, then squeeze them very well with your hands. Rinse and squeeze well again. Use some muscle—squeezing them really firmly is what helps to tenderize the noodles.

4. Add the noodles to the bowl and stir to combine thoroughly with the sauce and veggies. Serve at room temperature or cold. Do not reheat. Refrigerate in an airtight container for up to 5 days.

Ingredient tip: You can find kelp noodles in the refrigerated section at health food stores or online.

Per serving: Calories: 190; Fat: 7g; Carbohydrates: 25g; Fiber: 4g; Protein: 9g; Sodium: 963mg; Iron: 4mg

NOODLES AND RICE

WORLD'S HEALTHIEST MAC AND CHEESE

SERVES 4

Prep Time: 10 minutes
Cook Time: 20 minutes

○ 30 MINUTES OR LESS
● GLUTEN-FREE
○ WFPB

2 cups gold or russet potatoes, peeled and cut into ½-inch pieces

1 cup carrot, cut into ½-inch pieces

½ cup raw cashews

½ cup water

¼ cup plus 2 tablespoons nutritional yeast

3 tablespoons mellow white miso

3 tablespoons freshly squeezed lime juice

4 large garlic cloves, peeled

1 tablespoon onion granules or powder

1 teaspoon dried rosemary

½ teaspoon freshly ground black pepper

2 cups chopped broccoli florets

8 ounces brown rice rotini pasta

½ cup Plantstrong Parm (page 200) (optional, but highly recommended)

───────────

Meal prep it: If you're like me, you'll want to make it extra easy to whip this up on busy nights. To do so, simply chop your broccoli ahead of time and store it in the refrigerator in an airtight container. Make the sauce in advance and store it in the refrigerator as well. Then, when you're ready for dinner, gently reheat the sauce, make the pasta, and steam the broccoli.

Per serving: Calories: 397; Fat: 8g; Carbohydrates: 68g; Fiber: 8g; Protein: 16g; Sodium: 521mg; Iron: 4mg

This pasta dish is as healthy as can be, but don't let that fool you into thinking it's not delicious. This is a crowd-pleaser in our household, for even the pickiest of kids (I'm looking at you, Alethea). It's chock-full of immune-boosting properties (hey there, garlic and miso), high in B12, and nutrient-dense. Here's to excellent health!

1. Fill a large pot with a few inches of water and bring to a boil. Place the potatoes, carrots, and cashews in a steaming basket inside the pot, cover, reduce the heat to low, and steam for 20 minutes, or until the potatoes and carrots are tender.

2. In a blender, combine the steamed veggies and cashews, water, nutritional yeast, miso, lime juice, garlic, onion granules, rosemary, and pepper. Blend until completely smooth. Set aside.

3. In the same steamer basket over low heat, steam the broccoli for 3 to 5 minutes, or until tender. You may need to add more water to the pot if it all evaporated during the first steam. If so, bring to a boil again, then reduce heat to low. Set the broccoli aside.

4. Bring a large pot of water to a boil and cook the pasta according to the directions on the package. Once al dente, drain.

5. Gently toss the pasta with the sauce and broccoli. Serve immediately, topped with the Plantstrong Parm (if using).

7-Layer Dip, page 156

CHAPTER TEN

SPECIAL OCCASION SHOWSTOPPERS

7-LAYER DIP

SERVES 6 TO 8

Prep Time: 5 minutes
Cook Time: 2 minutes

- GLUTEN-FREE
- PLAN AHEAD

2 (15-ounce) cans fat-free vegan refried beans

Low-Fat Cheese Dip (page 208)

4 cups shredded or finely chopped romaine lettuce

2 cups Classic Salsa (page 202)

Chipotle Cream Sauce (page 206)

Classic Guacamole (page 64)

2 medium tomatoes, chopped

Tortilla chips, for serving

Who says you can't make a healthy, vegan, and totally delicious version of 7-layer dip? Not me—I don't spread those types of false rumors. Enjoy this dip for special occasions, or even as an extra-fun weeknight dinner (yes, I meant to say dinner). With some healthy whole-grain tortilla chips (or home-baked ones), this is a totally legit entrée.

1. In a medium pot, heat the refried beans on the stove over low heat, stirring often, until hot. You may need to add a little water to thin. This should take about 2 minutes.

2. Spread the beans over the bottom of an 8-by-10-inch dish. Top evenly with the Low-Fat Cheese Dip. Sprinkle with the lettuce, distributing it evenly. Pour the Classic Salsa over the top. Evenly drizzle the Chipotle Cream Sauce over the salsa and scoop the Classic Guacamole on top. The guacamole may not spread over the entire layer of dip—it's okay if it's in dollops. Sprinkle the tomatoes on top and serve immediately, with tortilla chips for dipping.

Make it WFPB: Omit the salt from the recipes and use baked tortilla chips for dipping.

Meal prep it: Almost everything in this recipe can be prepared in advance. Make the cheese dip, salsa, and chipotle sauce up to a week in advance. Chop the lettuce and tomatoes the day beforehand. You can even make the guacamole several hours in advance (but not much more, for optimal freshness). Then, actual prep time for this dish will only be about 5 minutes.

Per serving: Calories: 356; Fat: 14g; Carbohydrates: 45g; Fiber: 13g; Protein: 16g; Sodium: 635mg; Iron: 5mg

LOADED CHEESY FRIES

SERVES 4

Prep Time: 20 minutes
Cook Time: 30 minutes

GLUTEN-FREE
PLAN AHEAD

FOR THE FRIES

4 medium gold or russet potatoes (skins on)

2 teaspoons neutral-flavored oil (avocado, sunflower, or sesame)

2 teaspoons garlic granules or powder

1 teaspoon paprika

½ teaspoon sea salt

FOR THE TOPPINGS

Nonstick cooking spray (coconut or avocado oil)

4 strips tempeh bacon

2 teaspoons neutral-flavored oil (avocado, sunflower, or sesame)

1 cup thinly sliced shallots

1 cup prepared Cheesy Sauce (page 210)

¼ cup minced scallions or chives, both green and white parts

1 jalapeño, thinly sliced (optional)

Cashew Ranch Dressing (page 205), for dipping (optional)

Make it WFPB: Omit the salt from the fries, cheese sauce, and ranch dressing. Bake the potatoes on silicone liners or a nonstick pan and omit the oil. Sauté the shallots in water instead of oil.

Per serving: Calories: 293; Fat: 7g; Carbohydrates: 51g; Fiber: 6g; Protein: 10g; Sodium: 555mg; Iron: 3mg

These over-the-top fries are absolutely scrumptious and so fun to eat. Plus, they're actually good for you. Try making them in an air fryer!

TO MAKE THE FRIES

1. Cut the potatoes lengthwise into ½-inch-thick slices. Next, cut each slice into sticks that resemble the shape of french fries. Keep them as uniform as possible so they cook evenly.

2. Preheat the oven to 400°F. In a large bowl, place the potatoes, oil, garlic granules, paprika, and salt. Toss well to coat.

3. Transfer the potatoes to a large baking sheet, spreading them out over the pan so that none are overlapping. Bake for 10 to 15 minutes. Turn them over and bake for another 10 to 15 minutes, or until tender and golden brown on both sides.

TO MAKE THE TOPPINGS

1. To make the bacon, spray a small baking sheet with cooking spray. Place the tempeh bacon strips in a single layer on the sheet and spray with oil. Bake for 10 minutes, or until crisp and browned. Remove and set aside.

2. Meanwhile, make the caramelized shallots: In a medium skillet, heat the oil over medium-high heat and add the shallots. Cook for 10 to 15 minutes, stirring often, until the shallots are well browned. Set aside.

3. To assemble, place the fries on individual plates and top generously with Cheesy Sauce. Top equally with the caramelized shallots and crumble the tempeh bacon evenly over that. Garnish with scallions and jalapeño (if using), and use the Cashew Ranch Dressing (if using) for dipping. Enjoy immediately.

TOFU FANTASY

SERVES 4

Prep Time: 20 minutes
Cook Time: 20 minutes

● GLUTEN-FREE
● LEFTOVER-FRIENDLY
○ NUT-FREE
● PLAN AHEAD

FOR THE BROWN SAUCE

¾ cup water

½ cup coconut sugar

¼ cup tamari, shoyu, or soy sauce

¼ cup toasted sesame oil

5 large garlic cloves, minced or pressed

1½ tablespoons arrowroot powder

FOR THE SESAME TOFU

1 pound extra-firm tofu

1 teaspoon garlic granules or powder

3 tablespoons tamari, shoyu, or soy sauce

¾ cup sesame seeds

3 tablespoons brown rice flour or whole wheat pastry flour

3 tablespoons neutral-flavored oil (sunflower, avocado, raw sesame), divided

4 cups cooked brown rice (see page 18)

1 teaspoon toasted sesame oil

4 cups broccoli florets

1 large carrot, peeled and thinly sliced

3 cups finely diced zucchini

1 cup baby corn or corn kernels

Fantasy might be a strong word, but based on my extensive market research (a.k.a. making this for my daughter and her friends a million times), this tofu dish is what dreams are made of. Turn to it when you're craving Chinese takeout—it's equally as delicious, and obviously much healthier. You'll likely have extra sauce, but it'll last for up to a month in your refrigerator and makes weeknight meals a snap when you want a stir-fry with pizzazz.

TO MAKE THE BROWN SAUCE

1. In a medium pan, combine the water, coconut sugar, tamari, oil, and garlic over medium-high heat. Cook for 1 to 2 minutes or until hot.

2. Transfer about ¼ cup to a bowl and whisk it with the arrowroot powder until smooth. Add back to the pan and whisk it into the mixture.

3. Reduce the heat to medium-low and continue to cook for 3 minutes, whisking constantly, just until thickened (don't overcook). Set aside.

TO MAKE THE SESAME TOFU

1. Cut the tofu horizontally into 8 slabs. Press the tofu (see page 14), then cut the tofu slabs into 2-inch triangles. Place the pieces in a single layer on a large plate or pan.

2. Sprinkle the garlic granules and tamari evenly over the tofu, turning the pieces to coat all sides. Place the seeds and flour in a large plastic bag and shake well to combine. Place half of the tofu triangles into the bag and gently shake to thoroughly coat each piece with the breading.

3. In a large skillet or wok, heat 1½ tablespoons of oil over medium-high heat. Once hot, place the coated tofu pieces in a single layer into the pan. Cook for 3 to 5 minutes, or until the undersides are golden brown. Flip each piece over and cook for another 3 to 5 minutes, or until both sides are golden brown. Move to a plate. Repeat the breading and cooking steps with the remaining tofu and 1½ tablespoons oil.

4. Meanwhile, in a large skillet or wok, heat the sesame oil over medium-high heat and add the broccoli, carrot, and zucchini. Stir-fry for 5 minutes, or until the vegetables are tender but still slightly crisp. Add the corn and cook an additional minute, until heated through.

5. Place the rice in bowls and top with the vegetables and tofu. Drizzle with sauce and serve immediately.

Make it WFPB: Omit the oil from the sauce and add ¼ cup toasted sesame seeds. If necessary, add a little water to thin. For the tofu, you can skip pan-frying it and instead bake it at 400°F for 30 to 40 minutes (or until browned), turning each piece over about halfway through. Stir-fry the vegetables in water instead of oil.

Variation tip: Feel free to vary the vegetables any way you like—pea pods, mushrooms, and red bell peppers are all great choices. You can also use either variety of Peanut Sauce, Two Ways (page 207) instead of the Brown Sauce.

Per serving: Calories: 848; Fat: 44g; Carbohydrates: 90g; Fiber: 14g; Protein: 28g; Sodium: 2288mg; Iron: 6mg

GOLDEN TOFU WITH COCONUT-LIME QUINOA

SERVES 4

Prep Time: 10 minutes

Cook Time: 25 minutes

- ◐ 30 MINUTES OR LESS
- ◑ GLUTEN-FREE
- ● LEFTOVER-FRIENDLY
- ○ NUT-FREE

FOR THE COCONUT-LIME QUINOA

1 (13.5-ounce) can full-fat coconut milk

1 cup quinoa

¼ cup freshly squeezed lime juice

3 tablespoons minced scallions, both green and white parts

2 tablespoons grated fresh ginger

½ teaspoon sea salt

FOR THE GOLDEN TOFU

1 pound firm tofu

1 tablespoon ground cumin

1 tablespoon ground coriander

2 teaspoons garlic granules or powder

½ teaspoon ground turmeric

¼ teaspoon ground cayenne

2 tablespoons tamari, shoyu, or soy sauce

2 tablespoons freshly squeezed lime juice

¼ cup plus 2 tablespoons chickpea flour

2 tablespoons neutral-flavored oil (sunflower, avocado, or raw sesame), divided

½ teaspoon sea salt

1 teaspoon black sesame seeds (optional)

¼ cup chopped fresh cilantro or cilantro microgreens

Everything from the ultra-creamy, tangy quinoa (with the perfect ginger kick) to the spicy, crispy tofu will make you wish you didn't have people over, trying to eat some of your wannabe future leftovers. Yes, it's nice to share. But also, sometimes you just don't want to, and that's okay. Serve this tasty treasure with the Spinach Salad with Sesame-Ginger-Orange Dressing (page 83) and some Edamame Miso Hummus (page 66) or Luscious Eggplant (page 71) for a truly epic meal.

TO MAKE THE COCONUT-LIME QUINOA

1. In a medium pot, combine the coconut milk, quinoa, and lime juice over high heat. Cover and bring to a boil.

2. Reduce the heat to low and simmer for 15 minutes, mostly covered, until the quinoa is tender and most of the liquid has been absorbed.

3. Stir in the scallions, ginger, and ½ teaspoon salt. Set aside.

TO MAKE THE GOLDEN TOFU

1. Slice the tofu into ½-inch-thick horizontal slabs and press the tofu (see page 14). Cut into ½-inch-thick cubes.

2. In a medium bowl, combine the cumin, coriander, garlic granules, turmeric, and cayenne, and stir well. Add the tofu and toss to coat. Drizzle the tamari and lime juice over the tofu and stir gently with a rubber spatula. Sprinkle the chickpea flour onto the tofu, and gently stir or shake to coat the tofu evenly.

CONTINUED ▶

3. Heat a large wok or skillet over medium-high heat and add 1 tablespoon oil. Once hot, add half of the tofu and cook for 5 to 6 minutes, flipping once or twice, until the tofu is evenly browned. Transfer the tofu to a plate and repeat with the remaining oil and tofu. Sprinkle the tofu evenly with the salt.

4. To serve, scoop the quinoa onto plates (you can even use a ½ cup measuring cup or small bowl as a mold, for added fanciness) and sprinkle with the sesame seeds (if using). Serve the tofu alongside the quinoa, and top everything with the cilantro. Enjoy immediately. Refrigerate leftovers in an airtight container for 3 to 4 days.

Make it WFPB: Omit the salt. Bake the tofu at 400°F for 30 minutes, or until browned, on a silicone liner or nonstick baking sheet instead of pan-frying in oil.

Per serving: Calories: 658; Fat: 30g; Carbohydrates: 45g; Fiber: 7g; Protein: 20g; Sodium: 548mg; Iron: 5mg

PEANUTTY QUINOA WITH LEMONGRASS TOFU

SERVES 4

Prep Time: 20 minutes, plus marinating time

Cook Time: 45 minutes

○ GLUTEN-FREE
● LEFTOVER-FRIENDLY
○ PLAN AHEAD

FOR THE LEMONGRASS TOFU

1 pound extra-firm tofu

½ cup chopped carrot

½ cup chopped onion

½ cup water

¼ cup chopped fresh lemongrass

¼ cup mellow white miso

2 tablespoons freshly squeezed lime juice

2 tablespoons tamari, shoyu, or soy sauce

1 tablespoon toasted sesame oil

FOR THE PEANUTTY QUINOA

2 tablespoons maple syrup

2 teaspoons toasted sesame oil

2 tablespoons smooth peanut butter

2 tablespoons tamari, shoyu, or soy sauce

2 tablespoons freshly squeezed lime juice

3 large garlic cloves, pressed or minced

½ cup chopped fresh cilantro

⅓ cup finely diced carrot

3 cups cooked quinoa (see page 18)

¼ cup crushed dry-roasted peanuts, for garnish

¼ cup basil microgreens, for garnish

This delectable dish is a party in your mouth and a feast for your eyes. I love the variation of textures—from the soft, silky tofu to the crunch of the carrots and peanuts, to the airy microgreens on top. If you have trouble finding basil microgreens, you can substitute another variety (such as cilantro), or just sprinkle a little fresh basil on top. For an absolute feast, serve this with Maple Shishitos (page 67), Chili-Ginger Cabbage (page 75), and Lemon-Ginger Miso Soup (page 101).

TO MAKE THE LEMONGRASS TOFU

1. Press the tofu (see page 14). I recommend pressing for at least 30 minutes for this dish.

2. In a blender, combine the carrot, onion, water, lemongrass, miso, lime juice, tamari, and oil until very smooth. Pour the mixture into a large baking dish. Cut the tofu into eight horizontal slabs and then into squares, to form 16 tofu squares that are about 2 inches wide and ½ inch thick. Place the tofu into the sauce in a single layer and gently turn to coat on all sides. Marinate the tofu for several hours or up to 2 days. Turn once or twice while marinating so that the tofu absorbs as much sauce as possible.

3. Preheat the oven to 400°F. Line a baking sheet with a silicone liner or parchment paper.

4. Place the tofu on the prepared baking sheet. Scoop any additional sauce onto the tofu. Bake for 20 minutes. Remove, flip each piece over gently with a spatula, and bake for another 20 to 25 minutes, or until golden brown. Remove and set aside.

CONTINUED ▶

TO MAKE THE PEANUTTY QUINOA

1. In a medium-large bowl, place the maple syrup, sesame oil, peanut butter, and tamari. Whisk until smooth. Whisk in the lime juice and garlic and then add the cilantro and carrot. Add the quinoa to the bowl and toss gently with a rubber spatula until the quinoa is thoroughly coated in the sauce.

2. To serve, divide the quinoa evenly in between bowls and top each bowl with 4 pieces of tofu. Sprinkle the peanuts onto the quinoa, and place the microgreens on top. Refrigerate leftovers in an airtight container for 3 to 4 days.

Make it WFPB: Omit the toasted sesame oil.

Per serving: Calories: 507; Fat: 21g; Carbohydrates: 54g; Fiber: 9g; Protein: 25g; Sodium: 1672mg; Iron: 13mg

CHICKPEA POTATO CURRY

SERVES 6 TO 8

Prep Time: 10 minutes
Cook Time: About 40 minutes

- GLUTEN-FREE
- LEFTOVER-FRIENDLY
- NUT-FREE

2 tablespoons oil (sunflower, coconut, non-virgin olive, or safflower)

1½ tablespoons black mustard seeds

1½ tablespoons cumin seeds

1 tablespoon ground cumin

1 tablespoon ground coriander

¾ teaspoon asafetida powder

¾ teaspoon red pepper flakes

¾ teaspoon dried turmeric

1¼ cups diced onion

1 (13.5-ounce) can full-fat coconut milk, divided

2 cups diced potatoes (skins on)

1 (15-ounce) can cooked chickpeas (1½ cups), drained and rinsed

1 (14.5-ounce) can diced tomatoes

3 tablespoons freshly squeezed lemon juice

5 large garlic cloves, pressed or minced

2 teaspoons sea salt

1 cup chopped fresh cilantro, for garnish (optional)

The complex, rich flavor of this curry is absolutely divine—and if you're a fan of authentic Indian cuisine, it will make your knees buckle. I like to serve this on top of basmati rice with some Red Lentil Dal (page 108) on the side.

1. In a large skillet or wok, heat the oil over medium-high heat. Add the mustard and cumin seeds and cook for 1 minute, stirring constantly, just until they begin to pop. Add the ground cumin, coriander, asafetida, red pepper flakes, and turmeric and cook for another minute, while stirring.

2. Add the onion and cook for 5 minutes or until softened, stirring often. As you go, add a little of the coconut milk so that the mixture does not become too dry.

3. Add the potatoes, chickpeas, remaining coconut milk, and the tomatoes and their juices. Stir well and bring to a boil.

4. Reduce the heat to medium-low and simmer for 25 to 35 minutes, or until the potatoes are tender and the sauce has thickened. Be sure to stir every few minutes during this process.

5. Stir the lemon juice, garlic, and salt into the curry until thoroughly combined. Serve by itself or over rice, with a sprinkling of cilantro (if using). Refrigerate leftovers in an airtight container for up to a week. They also freeze well, in an airtight container, for several months.

Ingredient tip: You can find asafetida at Indian markets, online, or international supermarkets. It's very unique in flavor, but if you can't find it, you can omit it and add another large clove (or two) of garlic instead.

Make it WFPB: Omit the salt and substitute coconut milk for oil.

Per serving: Calories: 200; Fat: 12g; Carbohydrates: 15g; Fiber: 2g; Protein: 1g; Sodium: 154mg; Iron: 2mg

SOUTHWEST SPRING ROLLS WITH GREEN CHILI SAUCE

MAKES 8 SPRING ROLLS

Prep Time: 15 minutes
Cook Time: 10 minutes

○ 30 MINUTES OR LESS
● GLUTEN-FREE

FOR THE GREEN CHILI SAUCE

1 teaspoon neutral-flavored oil (avocado, sunflower, or safflower)

1½ tablespoons brown rice flour or whole-wheat pastry flour

1½ cups roasted, peeled, and chopped mild green chilies, or 1 (13-ounce) container frozen green chilies, thawed

2 teaspoons coconut sugar

¼ cup plus 1 teaspoon freshly squeezed lime juice

5 medium garlic cloves, minced or pressed

1 to 1¼ teaspoons sea salt

FOR THE ROLLS

⅓ cup pine nuts

8 spring roll rice paper wraps (preferably made from brown rice)

1 ripe avocado, chopped

½ cup grated or julienned carrot

½ cup packed chopped fresh cilantro

4 scallions, both green and white parts, minced

First-timer tip: Don't overfill the wraps or they'll break. If they do, you can double-wrap them, or patch with another piece of softened spring roll wrapper.

Per serving: Calories: 130; Fat: 7g; Carbohydrates: 17g; Fiber: 2g; Protein: 2g; Sodium: 45mg; Iron: 2mg

Because of my undying obsession with spring rolls, I've created dozens of variations on them, but this is an absolute favorite. I adore the way the creamy avocado pairs with the crunchy toasted pine nuts and the tanginess of the green chili sauce. These are perfect served with Tempeh Corn Chili (page 106) or the Bean and Rice Bowl with Mango Salsa (page 139).

TO MAKE THE GREEN CHILI SAUCE

1. In a small pot, heat the oil and flour over medium heat. Stir well. Add the chilies and sugar, and increase the heat to medium-high. Cook for 5 minutes, stirring often, until slightly thickened.

2. Remove from the heat and stir in the lime juice, garlic, and salt. Set aside.

TO MAKE THE ROLLS

1. In a nonstick or steel pan, toast the nuts over low heat for 2 to 3 minutes, or until lightly browned and aromatic, shaking the pan often. Watch them closely, as they burn easily. Remove from heat and set aside.

2. Gently take a rice paper wrap and run it under warm water until thoroughly moistened on both sides. Lay flat on a nonporous surface. Place a small amount of pine nuts, avocado, carrot, cilantro, and scallions onto the wrapper in a horizontal line toward the bottom.

3. Once the rice paper is fully softened, roll the bottom of the wrapper up and over the fillings. Next, fold the left and right sides together, maintaining parallel lines, then roll all the way up from the bottom. The rice paper will self-seal. Set aside and repeat this process until all of the fillings are used. Serve with the green chili sauce.

BEET-CRUST PIZZA WITH CASHEW-MACADAMIA CHEESE

SERVES 4

Prep Time: 20 minutes
Cook Time: 40 minutes

- GLUTEN-FREE
- LEFTOVER-FRIENDLY
- PLAN AHEAD

FOR THE CRUST

Nonstick cooking spray (coconut or avocado oil)

1½ cups chickpea flour

1 cup finely grated, peeled beets

½ cup polenta meal

1 tablespoon olive oil

1 tablespoon water

2 teaspoons dried oregano

1 teaspoon garlic granules or powder

½ teaspoon sea salt

FOR THE PIZZA

1 cup vegan pasta sauce or pizza sauce of choice

1 cup thinly sliced kale leaves

½ cup diced onion

¼ cup sliced pitted kalamata olives

½ cup Cashew-Macadamia Cheese (page 204)

¼ cup thinly sliced basil, for garnish

¼ cup Plantstrong Parm (page 200), for garnish

HEALTHY VEGAN, HAPPY BODY

My cousin Stacia and I used to visit a restaurant in Grand Rapids, Michigan, for their beet-crust pizza because of how tasty, healthy, and innovative it was. That restaurant no longer exists, but do you know what's super cool? Stacia helped me re-create the recipe while she was visiting recently. We both agree that this version is even better than the one we used to get in Michigan. What's not to love about a pizza that's high-level healthy, vegan, and totally delicious? Not much, that's what.

TO MAKE THE CRUST

1. Preheat the oven to 400°F. Lightly spray a standard-size pizza pan with cooking spray. Set aside.

2. In a large bowl, combine the chickpea flour, beets, polenta, oil, water, oregano, garlic granules, and salt. Stir very well until thoroughly combined.

3. Place on the pizza pan and, using your hands, press out to evenly cover the entire pan, making a small raised crust around the edges, if desired. Moisten your hands once or twice during this process so the crust doesn't stick to your hands. Bake for 15 minutes, or until just barely beginning to brown in parts, and remove from the oven.

TO MAKE THE PIZZA

1. To make the pizza, evenly spread the pizza sauce over the crust and then top with the kale, onion, and olives. Spoon the cheese over the top and bake for another 25 minutes, or until the cheese begins to slightly brown and the kale has dried.

2. Remove from the oven and evenly top with the basil and Plantstrong Parm. Cut into 8 pieces and serve immediately. Refrigerate leftovers in an airtight container for up to 5 days. Reheat in a toaster oven, oven, or air fryer to maintain the texture of the crust.

Make it WFPB: Omit the salt and use extra water instead of olive oil for the crust.

Fun fact: Once, when Stacia and I were visiting that pizza place, we asked them what exactly was in their beet crust. Their reply? "Just beets." Yeah, we didn't believe them either. Luckily, we both have the ability to decipher ingredients by tasting them and added a few extras to this version to make it even better.

Per serving (2 slices): Calories: 206; Fat: 13g; Carbohydrates: 17g; Fiber: 4g; Protein: 8g; Sodium: 75mg; Iron: 2mg

ENCHILADA CASSEROLE

SERVES 8 TO 10

Prep Time: 20 minutes, plus at least 2 hours for chilling

Cook Time: 40 minutes

- GLUTEN-FREE
- ● LEFTOVER-FRIENDLY
- PLAN AHEAD

FOR THE POLENTA

3 cups water

1 cup dry polenta meal

3 tablespoons nutritional yeast

¾ teaspoon sea salt

FOR THE CASSEROLE

2 (15-ounce) cans pinto beans, drained and rinsed, or 3 cups cooked pinto beans (see page 17), divided

1¾ cups minced yellow or white onion, divided

2 cups lightly packed baby spinach

1 (12-ounce) jar green tomatillo sauce

12 corn tortillas (preferably sprouted), divided

2 (14-ounce) cans vegan enchilada sauce, divided

½ lime, juiced

3 medium tomatillos, thinly sliced

1½ cups prepared Cheesy Sauce (page 210)

¾ cup chopped pitted kalamata olives

2 scallions, both green and white parts, minced, for garnish

½ cup minced fresh cilantro, for garnish

My friend Annie called me the other day in a panic looking for a knockout vegan dish to serve a big group. I recommended this delicious bake because I've relied on it more times than I can count to please a crowd. Luckily, it was a hit at her event, too! Even non-vegans will love this. Feel free to make it even easier by substituting a shredded vegan cheese (such as Parmela or Violife) for the Cheesy Sauce. Serve this alongside some tortilla chips dipped in Classic Salsa (page 202), Classic Guacamole (page 64), or Low-Fat Cheese Dip (page 208).

TO MAKE THE POLENTA

1. In a medium pot, combine the water and polenta over medium-high heat. Cook until it begins to thicken, whisking continuously.

2. Turn the heat to the lowest possible setting and continue to cook for 5 to 10 minutes or until very thick, whisking constantly. Stir in the nutritional yeast and salt.

3. Remove from heat and transfer to a large, lightly oiled baking pan (at least 9.5-by-13.5 inches). With the palms of your hands, press the layer of polenta as flat as possible. Cover and allow to chill in the refrigerator for several hours or overnight, until very firm.

TO MAKE THE CASSEROLE

1. Preheat the oven to 400°F.

2. Remove the polenta from the refrigerator and evenly scatter half of the beans and half of the onion over the top of it. Place the spinach on top of the beans and onion. Pour the tomatillo sauce on top of the spinach in an even layer.

3. Place 6 of the tortillas in a (relatively) single layer on top of the spinach and sauce. Cover the tortillas evenly with the remaining beans and onions. Pour 1 can enchilada sauce evenly on top of that. Drizzle the sauce with the juice of ½ lime.

4. Layer in the remaining six tortillas and top with the remaining can of enchilada sauce. Place the tomatillos evenly on top and drizzle with Cheesy Sauce. Scatter the olives on top of that.

5. Cover the pan with aluminum foil and bake for 30 minutes, then uncover and bake for another 10 minutes, or until golden brown and bubbly. Serve immediately, topped with the scallions and cilantro. Refrigerate leftovers for about a week or freeze for up to 4 months.

Ingredient tip: Remove the papery skin from the outside of the tomatillos before you slice them.

Make it WFPB: Omit the salt.

Per serving: Calories: 246; Fat: 7g; Carbohydrates: 39g; Fiber: 9g; Protein: 9g; Sodium: 707mg; Iron: 3mg

**Raspberry
Chocolate
Cheesecake,**
page 193

CHAPTER ELEVEN

DESSERTS

PEANUT BUTTER OATMEAL ENERGY COOKIES

MAKES ABOUT 24 COOKIES

Prep Time: 15 minutes

○ 30 MINUTES OR LESS
◑ GLUTEN-FREE
● LEFTOVER-FRIENDLY

2 cups rolled oats

½ cup dry-roasted unsalted organic peanuts

½ cup packed raisins

¼ cup smooth peanut butter

¼ cup maple syrup

2 tablespoons water

2 tablespoons chia seeds

1 tablespoon vanilla extract

¾ teaspoon sea salt

No-bake cookies that are chock-full of super-charging ingredients are totally my jam! Not only are they easy to make and nutrient-dense (as well as delicious), they're also the perfect travel staple. We always bring some sort of energy cookie during our travels, whether on road trips or flights—they're even great for just scooting around town. When I'm running errands and a little hungry, even one of these cookies boosts my energy and happily gets me to the next meal.

1. In a food processor, combine the oats, peanuts, raisins, peanut butter, maple syrup, water, chia seeds, vanilla, and salt and blend until sticky. You'll know the mixture is done blending when it balls up and starts to stick together, but a little texture still remains.

2. Using your hands, roll the mixture into 1-inch balls. Refrigerate in an airtight container for up to a month.

Variation tip: If you like, you can roll these cookies in raw cacao nibs for a chocolaty twist.

Per serving (1 cookie): Calories: 134; Fat: 8g; Carbohydrates: 12g; Fiber: 2g; Protein: 5g; Sodium: 4mg; Iron: 1mg

FLOURLESS PECAN COOKIES

MAKES ABOUT 24 COOKIES

Prep Time: 10 minutes
Cook Time: 10 minutes

- GLUTEN-FREE
- LEFTOVER-FRIENDLY
- PLAN AHEAD

1½ cups raw pecan halves, plus more for garnish

½ cup, packed pitted dates (5 large dates)

½ cup rolled oats

3 tablespoons maple syrup

1 teaspoon vanilla extract

½ teaspoon ground cinnamon

¼ teaspoon sea salt

¼ cup Buckwheat Crisps (page 199) or rolled oats

Substitution tip: If you don't have the Buckwheat Crisps on hand, you can stir in some additional rolled oats instead. They'll still be delicious, but won't have that extra crunch from the buckwheat.

Per serving (1 cookie): Calories: 74; Fat: 6g; Carbohydrates: 6g; Fiber: 1g; Protein: 1g; Sodium: 0mg; Iron: 0mg

These cookies are a nod to my darling grandma, who always had pecan cookies in her cookie jar. This version is not only packed with nutrition, it's addictively delicious and very easy to make. Plus, these cookies are another reason to keep Buckwheat Crisps (page 199) on hand, as they lend a nice crispy texture. They're especially delicious when fresh out of the oven and just slightly cooled, although they will last at room temperature for at least a week in an airtight container. We keep this cookie mix on hand (it'll last for weeks in the refrigerator) and bake them up whenever we need warm cookie love.

1. Preheat the oven to 350°F. Line two baking sheets with silicone mats or parchment paper and set aside.

2. In a food processor, blend the pecans, dates, oats, maple syrup, vanilla, cinnamon, and salt until thoroughly combined but not completely smooth. Transfer to a bowl and stir in the Buckwheat Crisps.

3. Scoop the dough out onto the cookie sheets in 1-inch balls, leaving a few inches in between each one. Wet a fork and press down on each cookie to compress it (and to leave a cute little fork print). Press a pecan half into the top of each cookie.

4. Bake for 10 minutes, or until lightly browned. Allow to cool slightly before transferring to a cooling rack or plate. Store in an airtight container at room temperature for up to a week.

SUGAR-FREE PEANUT BUTTER CHOCOLATE CUPS

MAKES 6 CHOCOLATE CUPS

Prep Time: 15 to 20 minutes
Cook Time: 2 to 3 minutes

- ○ 30 MINUTES OR LESS
- ◐ GLUTEN-FREE
- ● LEFTOVER-FRIENDLY

FOR THE CHOCOLATE LAYER

½ cup stevia-sweetened vegan chocolate chips (I use Lily's brand)

2 teaspoons refined coconut oil

2 teaspoons maple syrup

FOR THE PEANUT BUTTER LAYER

⅓ cup smooth unsalted unsweetened peanut butter

3 tablespoons maple syrup

1 teaspoon vanilla extract

¼ teaspoon plus ⅛ teaspoon sea salt

2 teaspoons crushed peanuts, unsalted (optional)

2 teaspoons cacao nibs (optional)

½ teaspoon chia seeds (optional)

Why make your own peanut butter cups? Good question. Personally, I prefer sugar-free treats, and I haven't found any on the market that I love. Hence, this ultra-yummy, naturally sweetened recipe was born. It's a quicker version than the traditionally enclosed kind—the chocolate and peanut butter are simply layered into the cups. But the shorter process means you can make it more often. How's that for a reason?

TO MAKE THE CHOCOLATE LAYER

1. Place muffin liners in six cups of a muffin tin and set aside.

2. In a small pot, combine the chocolate chips and oil over the lowest heat possible. Stir constantly until the chips become mostly melted. Remove from heat and stir until the chips are completely melted. It's important to heat the chocolate as minimally as possible to keep it from seizing. This should only take 2 to 3 minutes at the most.

3. Stir the maple syrup into the chocolate and evenly distribute the chocolate mixture into the bottom of each muffin cup. Using the back of a spoon or butter knife, spread it into a thin layer to thoroughly coat the bottom of all six muffin cups, using all the chocolate. Place in the refrigerator for about 5 minutes, or until the chocolate becomes firm.

TO MAKE THE PEANUT BUTTER LAYER

1. In a small bowl, mix the peanut butter, maple syrup, vanilla, and salt together until well combined.

2. Remove the cups from the refrigerator and top each chocolate layer evenly with the peanut butter mixture. If using, sprinkle the peanuts, cacao nibs, and/or chia seeds evenly over the peanut butter, and press down lightly to secure them.

3. Refrigerate for another 10 to 15 minutes, or until the chocolate is completely set. Serve cold or at room temperature. Refrigerate in an airtight container for up to a month—if you have more willpower than all other humans, that is.

_____

Make it WFPB: Omit the chocolate layer and simply top the peanut butter layer with chocolate chips and the cacao nibs, crushed peanuts, and chia seeds.

Per serving (1 chocolate cup): Calories: 155; Fat: 11g; Carbohydrates: 14g; Fiber: 3g; Protein: 4g; Sodium: 2mg; Iron: 1mg

RAW CHOCOLATE MINT TARTS

MAKES 12 SMALL TARTS

Prep Time: 30 minutes, plus
1 to 1½ hours for chilling

- ○ GLUTEN-FREE
- ● LEFTOVER-FRIENDLY
- ○ PLAN AHEAD

FOR THE CRUST

1 cup raw almonds

½ cup firmly packed pitted dates
(6 large dates)

2 tablespoons cacao powder

2 tablespoons cacao nibs

¼ teaspoon sea salt

1 tablespoon water

Nonstick cooking spray (coconut or
avocado oil)

FOR THE MINTY FILLING

1 cup raw unsalted whole cashews,
soaked, drained, and rinsed (see page 11)

½ cup maple syrup

⅓ cup loosely packed baby spinach leaves

2 tablespoons coconut oil

2 teaspoons vanilla extract

1 teaspoon mint extract

½ teaspoon sea salt

FOR THE CHOCOLATE DRIZZLE

¼ cup cacao powder

¼ cup maple syrup

1 tablespoon coconut oil, melted

1 teaspoon vanilla extract

¼ teaspoon sea salt

1 tablespoon cacao nibs, for garnish

These tarts are ridiculously yummy and easier to make than the list of ingredients suggests. Serve these whenever you want a delicious dessert that's free from refined flours and sugars.

1. To make the crust, in a food processor, combine the almonds, dates, cacao powder, cacao nibs, salt, and water. Blend until sticky and thoroughly combined. Spray the cups of a muffin tin and press the crust firmly into the bottoms of each cup (you'll use about 2 tablespoons per muffin cup). Place in the refrigerator or freezer.

2. To make the minty filling, in a blender or food processor, combine the cashews, maple syrup, spinach, oil, vanilla, mint, and salt and blend until completely smooth. Spoon evenly into the muffin tins, on top of the chocolate crusts. Place in the freezer for about an hour, until the filling is very firm.

3. Meanwhile, to make the chocolate drizzle, in a bowl, combine the cacao powder, maple syrup, oil, vanilla, and salt and whisk until completely smooth. Set aside.

4. Once the tart filling is very firm, remove from the freezer. Drizzle the tops of the tarts with the chocolate sauce and sprinkle evenly with cacao nibs. Place back into the freezer for 10 minutes, or until the chocolate is set and solid. Run a knife around the edges of each muffin cup and pop the tarts out. Serve immediately. Store any leftovers in the freezer for up to 4 months.

Make it WFPB: Omit the salt and use water in place of oil for the filling and omit the oil completely for the chocolate drizzle.

Ingredient tip: Depending on the water content of your spinach, the filling may be firm enough to simply refrigerate, but I recommend freezing leftovers and thawing them for 5 minutes before enjoying.

Per serving (1 tart): Calories: 265; Fat: 15g; Carbohydrates: 28g; Fiber: 4g; Protein: 6g; Sodium: 5mg; Iron: 2mg

MINT CHOCOLATE CHIP NICE CREAM

SERVES 4

Prep Time: 5 minutes

○ 30 MINUTES OR LESS
◐ GLUTEN-FREE
● LEFTOVER-FRIENDLY
○ NUT-FREE
○ WFPB

3 ripe peeled bananas, broken into chunks and frozen

1 large handful baby spinach

½ to 1 cup unsweetened plain or vanilla nondairy milk

½ teaspoon mint extract

¼ cup vegan chocolate chips

This dessert reminds me of my favorite childhood ice cream, yet it's infinitely healthier. My grandma and I would go on ice cream dates to Bonnie Doon, and I'd invariably get a cone filled with mint chocolate chip ice cream. I'm thrilled to be able to enjoy this version because it's not only vegan, but also ultra-nourishing and low in fat and even sneaks in some greens. Be sure to serve immediately, as nice cream isn't so nice if it sits out very long.

1. In a blender, combine the bananas, spinach, ½ cup of milk, and mint. Blend until very smooth, adding additional milk as needed—just enough to make your blender cooperate. Be careful not to add more milk than you need, or your nice cream will be runny.

2. Stir in the chocolate chips (I use the stevia-sweetened Lily's brand) and serve immediately. This doesn't freeze too well due to the lack of fat in the nice cream, so it's best eaten when freshly made.

First-timer tip: Be sure to wash your spinach well, as it can often harbor dirt particles, then pat dry so as not to add extra moisture to the dish. However, if you're buying triple-washed baby greens, you should be able to toss them right in without additional washing.

Ingredient tip: The exact amount of nondairy milk you'll need will depend on your blender and the size of your bananas. Start slow and use just enough to blend.

Per serving: Calories: 141; Fat: 4g; Carbohydrates: 27g; Fiber: 3g; Protein: 2g; Sodium: 30mg; Iron: 1mg

BANANA NICE CREAM 4 WAYS

SERVES 2 TO 3

Prep Time: 5 minutes

- ○ 30 MINUTES OR LESS
- ◑ GLUTEN-FREE
- ○ NUT-FREE
- ◑ PLAN AHEAD
- ○ WFPB

FOR THE BASIC NICE CREAM BASE

2 ripe peeled bananas, broken into chunks and frozen

¼ to ½ cup unsweetened nondairy milk

1 teaspoon vanilla extract

FOR CLASSIC NICE CREAM

⅛ teaspoon ground nutmeg

FOR PEANUT BUTTER CHOCOLATE NICE CREAM

1 tablespoon peanut butter (smooth or chunky)

2 tablespoons vegan chocolate chips

FOR CARAMEL ALMOND NICE CREAM

2 tablespoons brown rice syrup

2 tablespoons toasted almonds

FOR SUPERFOOD NICE CREAM

2 tablespoons cacao nibs

2 teaspoons chia seeds

1 teaspoon maca powder (optional)

This is as whole-foods dessert as you can get (aside from just eating a piece of fruit). Banana nice cream is classic and delicious to boot. If you have a Yonanas healthy dessert maker, you can omit the milk and just make this with bananas, stirring in the vanilla afterward. Have fun experimenting with the different topping variations, or come up with your own.

1. In a blender, combine the bananas, ¼ cup of milk, and vanilla. Blend until very smooth, adding additional milk as needed—just enough to make your blender cooperate. Be careful not to add more milk than you need, or your nice cream will be runny.

2. To make the nice cream variations, top with those ingredients and serve immediately.

Ingredient tip: Maca powder, made from maca root, is available in any health food store. It's known for its strengthening and energizing properties, which makes it a favorite among athletes. Brown rice syrup consists solely of brown rice and water, so it's a low glycemic, whole-foods sweetener. It's also delicious, and has a smooth, caramel-like flavor.

Per serving (Basic Nice Cream Base): Calories: 77; Fat: 1g; Carbohydrates: 18g; Fiber: 2g; Protein: 1g; Sodium: 15mg; Iron: 0mg

APPLE CRISP WITH CREAMY LEMON SAUCE

SERVES 6 TO 8

Prep Time: 10 minutes

○ GLUTEN-FREE
● LEFTOVER-FRIENDLY
○ PLAN AHEAD

3 large red apples, any variety,
finely chopped

2 tablespoons coconut sugar

½ teaspoon ground cinnamon

½ teaspoon freshly squeezed lemon juice

2 cups Superfood Granola (page 40)

Creamy Lemon Sauce, for serving
(page 46)

This dish is the epitome of a healthy dessert—yet it's still so delicious. If you dehydrate the Superfood Granola (page 40), it's all raw. But even if baked, this crisp contains loads of enzymes and nutrients. This dessert can also double as a yummy breakfast or mini-meal. If you prefer a more traditional apple pie–like texture, you can bake the apple mixture before serving. I don't peel my apples before chopping for added fiber and color in this dessert.

1. If you'd like to bake the apples, preheat the oven to 400°F.

2. In a medium bowl, toss the apples, sugar, cinnamon, and lemon juice. Stir well. If you prefer the crisp raw, serve immediately in individual portions topped evenly with granola and drizzled with sauce.

3. If baking, add 1 or 2 tablespoons of water to the apple mixture so it doesn't dry out. Mix well and transfer to a baking dish or pie pan and bake for 20 minutes, or until the apples are tender. Allow to cool slightly before topping with the Superfood Granola and Creamy Lemon Sauce and serving. Refrigerate leftovers in an airtight container for 2 to 3 days.

Make it WFPB: Substitute water for the oil in the Creamy Lemon Sauce and omit the salt in both the Creamy Lemon Sauce and Superfood Granola.

Per serving: Calories: 142; Fat: 5g; Carbohydrates: 23g; Fiber: 3g; Protein: 4g; Sodium: 1mg; Iron: 1mg

CARAMELIZED BANANAS WITH CREAMY CARDAMOM SAUCE

SERVES 4

Prep Time: 5 minutes
Cook Time: 6 to 10 minutes

- ○ 30 MINUTES OR LESS
- ◉ GLUTEN-FREE
- ○ NUT-FREE

FOR THE CREAMY CARDAMOM SAUCE

1 (12.3-ounce) container firm silken tofu

½ cup maple syrup

4 teaspoons neutral-tasting oil (sunflower, refined coconut, or avocado)

1 teaspoon vanilla extract

¼ teaspoon ground cardamom

¼ teaspoon ground cinnamon

⅛ teaspoon sea salt

FOR THE CARAMELIZED BANANAS

3 firm bananas (not overly ripe)

1 tablespoon coconut sugar

2 teaspoons neutral-tasting oil (sunflower, refined coconut, or avocado)

1 cup sliced strawberries, for garnish

I once made a version of this dessert at a cooking class where one of the students had boldly declared that she hated tofu and would never like anything tofu-related. Fast-forward about two hours into the class, and she was literally licking this tofu-based sauce off her plate! Yep, that made me pretty happy. This dessert is not only plate-lickingly delicious, it's also nutritious, easy to make, and impressive.

TO MAKE THE CREAMY CARDAMOM SAUCE

In a blender, combine the tofu, maple syrup, oil, vanilla, cardamom, cinnamon, and salt until very smooth. Set aside or refrigerate for up to a week.

TO MAKE THE CARAMELIZED BANANAS

1. Slice each banana in half lengthwise, then again widthwise so that you end up with 12 banana segments. Sprinkle the bananas evenly with the coconut sugar.

2. In a large skillet, heat the oil over medium-high heat. Place the banana pieces in a single layer in the pan and cook for 3 to 5 minutes, or until golden brown on the undersides. Gently flip over and cook for another 3 to 5 minutes, or until both sides are caramelized. Turn off the heat.

3. Spoon a heaping serving of the sauce onto a dessert plate. Top with banana segments and garnish with strawberry slices. Serve immediately.

Make it WFPB: Omit the oil in the sauce and pan-fry the bananas on a dry nonstick skillet.

Per serving: Calories: 321; Fat: 10g; Carbohydrates: 56g; Fiber: 4g; Protein: 6g; Sodium: 11mg; Iron: 1mg

DESSERTS

183

PEACH COBBLER

SERVES 6

Prep Time: 10 minutes
Cook Time: 40 minutes

● LEFTOVER-FRIENDLY
○ NUT-FREE

FOR THE CRUST

¾ cup whole-wheat pastry flour

1⅛ teaspoons baking powder

⅛ teaspoon sea salt

2 tablespoons neutral-flavored oil
(sunflower, refined coconut, or avocado)

2 tablespoons maple syrup

1 tablespoon unsweetened nondairy milk

FOR THE FILLING

5½ cups chopped ripe peaches

¼ cup plus 2 tablespoons maple syrup

3 to 4 tablespoons arrowroot powder

2¼ teaspoons freshly squeezed
lemon juice

1 teaspoon ground cinnamon

½ teaspoon ground nutmeg

¼ teaspoon sea salt

Long ago when I was a personal chef, I'd make this dessert regularly for my weight-loss clients, and they absolutely flipped for it! I still think of them when I make this, because it's a great reminder that you don't have to sacrifice flavor and fun when you're trying to eat healthier. Try doing variations of this cobbler using blueberries, raspberries, or apples.

1. Preheat the oven to 400°F.

2. Make the crust: In a medium bowl, combine the flour, baking powder, and salt. Separately, in a small bowl, mix the oil, maple syrup, and milk. Stir into the flour mixture *just* until well combined (do not overmix). Place the dough in an airtight container and refrigerate.

3. Make the filling: Place the peaches in a large, covered baking dish. Add the maple syrup, 3 tablespoons arrowroot powder, lemon juice, cinnamon, nutmeg, and salt, and stir gently to combine. Cover and bake for 15 minutes. Remove and stir. If the mixture looks too runny, add the additional tablespoon of arrowroot powder. Gently stir and bake for another 10 to 20 minutes, or until thickened. Transfer to a lightly oiled 8-inch pie pan and set aside.

4. Take the dough out of the refrigerator and form into a ball. Next, place it on wax paper. Place another piece of wax paper on top of the dough. Using a rolling pin, roll over the top of the wax paper to flatten the dough into a circle a little larger than the size of the pie pan.

5. Gently remove the top sheet of wax paper from the crust. Carefully flip the crust over and onto the peach mixture. Remove the second sheet of wax paper. Tuck the crust into the sides of the pan. If you like, go around the rim with a fork to make a decorative edge.

6. Bake for an additional 10 minutes, or until the crust is lightly browned. Remove and enjoy. Refrigerate leftovers in an airtight container for up to 5 days.

Make it WFPB: Substitute blended silken tofu or applesauce for the oil in the crust (in equal amounts). Omit the salt.

Per serving: Calories: 320; Fat: 6g; Carbohydrates: 67g;
Fiber: 8g; Protein: 5g; Sodium: 97mg; Iron: 2mg

FRESH PUMPKIN PIE

SERVES 8

Prep Time: 5 to 10 minutes

Cook Time: 1 hour 35 minutes to 2 hours

○ GLUTEN-FREE

● LEFTOVER-FRIENDLY

○ NUT-FREE

1 small pie pumpkin or 2 cups cooked, mashed pumpkin

9-inch whole grain or gluten-free piecrust

1 (12.3-ounce) package extra-firm silken tofu

¾ cup pure maple syrup

⅓ cup coconut sugar

1½ tablespoons pumpkin pie spice

¼ teaspoon sea salt

It's a bit more work to make a pie using fresh versus canned pumpkin, but I've found it's totally worth it for the beautifully bright flavor it lends. Of course, you can make your own crust from scratch, too, but to offset the effort of baking the pumpkin, I've opted for premade whole-grain crusts here. This pumpkin pie is special enough for Thanksgiving, yet healthy enough to eat for breakfast. For an extra treat, top with nondairy whipped cream.

1. Preheat the oven to 400°F.

2. Cut the pumpkin in half. With a large metal spoon, scoop out the seeds and remove all of the stringy pulp. Place the pumpkin, cut sides down, in a large baking dish. Pour enough water over the pumpkin so that there is about ½ inch of water in the dish.

3. Bake for 45 to 60 minutes, or until the pumpkin flesh is soft and tender when you prick it with a fork. Remove the pumpkin and allow it to cool slightly.

4. Place the piecrust in a pie dish and bake for about 5 minutes. Remove the crust, but leave the oven on.

5. When the pumpkin has cooled slightly, scoop out 2 cups of flesh and place in a food processor or blender. Freeze any unused portion of the pumpkin for future use (I recommend adding it to the batter for muffins or pancakes, or blending it into soup).

6. To the food processor, add the tofu, maple syrup, coconut sugar, pumpkin pie spice, and salt and blend until very smooth.

7. Pour the filling into the prebaked piecrust. Bake for 45 minutes, or until nicely browned. Allow to cool in the refrigerator for several hours before serving. Refrigerate, covered with wax paper, for 3 to 4 days.

Ingredient tip: Don't let those pumpkin seeds go to waste. We like to toss the rinsed (and de-gooped) pumpkin seeds with seasoned salt, garlic, and a little sunflower oil and bake them until golden brown. This usually takes 30 to 40 minutes at 350°F, and you'll want to stir every 10 minutes or so. But don't say I didn't warn you—once you try these, there's no going back to store-bought roasted pumpkin seeds. You'll be ruined forever by the good stuff.

Per serving: Calories: 166; Fat: 2g; Carbohydrates: 35g; Fiber: 1g; Protein: 4g; Sodium: 64mg; Iron: 2mg

EASY CHERRY TURNOVERS

SERVES 4

Prep Time: 10 minutes

Cook Time: 10 to 20 minutes

○ 30 MINUTES OR LESS
● LEFTOVER-FRIENDLY
○ NUT-FREE

Nonstick cooking spray (coconut, sunflower, or avocado oil)

1 cup pitted, chopped cherries (fresh or frozen)

¼ cup plus 2 tablespoons fruit-sweetened cherry jam

2½ teaspoons arrowroot powder

½ teaspoon vanilla extract

8 whole-wheat phyllo dough sheets (9-by-13-inches each), thawed

2 tablespoons brown rice syrup, or more to taste

Ingredient tip: Brown rice syrup is made simply from brown rice and water. It's a sweetener that's lower glycemic yet deliciously rich. To me, it almost has a mellow caramel flavor. You can find it at any health food store.

Make it WFPB: Omit the oil spray and line the baking sheets with silicone liners or parchment paper before placing the turnovers on. Follow the recipe without using the oil spray.

Per serving: Calories: 213; Fat: 1g; Carbohydrates: 46g; Fiber: 3g; Protein: 33g; Sodium: 470mg; Iron: 8mg

These turnovers seem impressive, but are actually very quick and easy to make. Ah yes, the perfect way to fool unsuspecting guests and make them feel unnecessarily indebted to you. It'll be our little secret.

1. Preheat the oven to 350°F. Spray a small baking sheet with cooking spray and set aside.

2. In a medium bowl, stir the cherries, jam, arrowroot, and vanilla well. Set aside.

3. Lay two sheets of phyllo (one on top of the other) on a clean, dry surface. Fold in half lengthwise to form a 4½-by-13-inch rectangle with the short side facing you. Place ¼ of the filling at the base of the phyllo rectangle. Working from the corner, fold the bottom left edge of the phyllo up and over the mixture to form a triangle. Repeat this motion from the opposite corner, continuing the triangle pattern. Keep folding into triangles until you run out of phyllo.

4. Place the turnover on the prepared baking sheet and spray with oil. Repeat this process to make the remaining turnovers.

5. Bake for 10 to 20 minutes, or until golden brown. Remove from the oven and drizzle with the brown rice syrup just before serving. Refrigerate leftovers in an airtight container for up to 5 days.

Variation tip: You can sprinkle the turnovers with coconut sugar for their last 5 to 10 minutes of baking and omit the brown rice syrup if you like. As another variation, substitute a different type of fruit (and coordinating jam flavor) for the cherries.

RAW BLUEBERRY PEACH COBBLER

SERVES 4

Prep Time: 15 minutes

○ 30 MINUTES OR LESS
◐ GLUTEN-FREE
● LEFTOVER-FRIENDLY

FOR THE TOPPING

1 cup raw walnuts

½ cup raisins

¼ cup unsweetened coconut flakes

2 tablespoons coconut sugar

¼ teaspoon ground cinnamon

¼ teaspoon sea salt

FOR THE FILLING

2 cups fresh blueberries, divided

4 ripe peaches, chopped

1 teaspoon coconut sugar

⅛ teaspoon ground nutmeg

I love, love, love a raw dessert. Why, you ask? Because raw desserts are easy to make (no cooking, obviously), vibrant, nutrient-dense, and generally consist of whole-food ingredients. Oh, and did I mention they're absolutely delicious? This cobbler is satisfying enough to serve for dessert, but healthy enough to enjoy for breakfast.

1. Make the topping: In a food processor, combine the walnuts, raisins, coconut, sugar, cinnamon, and salt. Blend just until crumbly (if you process too long, you'll end up with a paste, which is not what you want). Allow the mixture to retain some texture, but make sure it's thoroughly blended. Set aside.

2. Make the filling: In a medium bowl, mash half of the blueberries with a fork. Add the remaining blueberries (keep them whole), peaches, sugar, and nutmeg and stir.

3. Place the fruit mixture in bowls and sprinkle evenly with the topping. Serve immediately. Refrigerate leftovers in an airtight container for 3 to 4 days.

Batch cooking tip: If you love this dessert as much as we do (and that's a lot!), make up a double (or triple) batch of the topping and keep it in the refrigerator. Then, you can make up this dessert in no time, just by chopping up the fruit filling and adding the premade crumble.

Per serving: Calories: 407; Fat: 23g; Carbohydrates: 52g; Fiber: 8g; Protein: 7g; Sodium: 15mg; Iron: 2mg

APPLE PUFFS WITH CARAMEL SAUCE

SERVES 6

Prep Time: 10 minutes

Cook Time: 10 to 20 minutes

○ 30 MINUTES OR LESS
● LEFTOVER-FRIENDLY
○ NUT-FREE

FOR THE APPLE PUFFS

2 red apples, any variety, finely chopped

2 tablespoons coconut sugar

2 teaspoons ground cinnamon

1 teaspoon freshly squeezed lemon juice

⅛ teaspoon sea salt

Nonstick cooking spray (coconut, sunflower, or another neutral-flavored oil)

6 large or 12 small whole-wheat phyllo dough sheets, thawed

FOR THE CARAMEL SAUCE

2 tablespoons refined coconut oil

¼ cup coconut sugar

¼ cup maple syrup

3 tablespoons brown rice syrup

1 teaspoon vanilla extract

½ teaspoon sea salt

This is one of the most impressive desserts in my repertoire—yet it's so darn easy to make. It's perfect for special occasions and, in our house, often makes an appearance alongside the Fresh Pumpkin Pie (page 186) on Thanksgiving. But don't wait until the holidays. You can whip this delectable dessert up anytime—it only takes about 30 minutes to make and is absolutely worth every second.

TO MAKE THE APPLE PUFFS

1. In a medium bowl, combine the apples, sugar, cinnamon, lemon juice, and salt and stir well. Set aside.

2. Preheat the oven to 350°F. Spray a baking sheet with cooking spray and set aside.

3. Gently unwrap the phyllo dough and remove 6 large or 12 small sheets. Rewrap the remaining phyllo in airtight plastic and place back in the refrigerator or freezer.

4. Remove 1 large or 2 small sheet(s) phyllo and place on a clean, dry surface. If you are using two small sheets, place one on top of the other. Spray the phyllo with oil. Fold the phyllo dough into thirds (the long way) so that it resembles a tall, skinny rectangle. The short side should be facing you.

5. Place about one-sixth of the apple mixture at the base of the phyllo rectangle. Working from the corner, fold the bottom left edge of the phyllo up and over the mixture to form a triangle. Repeat this motion from the opposite corner, continuing the triangle pattern. Keep folding into triangles until you run out of phyllo. Place on the prepared baking sheet and spray with oil. Repeat with the remaining phyllo sheets and apple mixture.

6. Bake for 10 to 20 minutes, or until golden brown.

CONTINUED ▶

DESSERTS

APPLE PUFFS WITH CARAMEL SAUCE — CONTINUED

TO MAKE THE CARAMEL SAUCE

1. While the puffs are baking, in a skillet, heat the oil over medium heat. Once it melts, whisk in the sugar, maple syrup, brown rice syrup, vanilla, and salt and reduce heat to low. Gently boil, stirring often, for about 2 minutes, or until thickened.

2. Serve each apple puff drizzled with caramel sauce. Refrigerate leftovers in an airtight container for 3 to 4 days.

Make it WFPB: Omit the oil spray and place the turnovers on baking pans lined with silicone liners or parchment paper. Proceed with the recipe without using the oil spray. For the caramel sauce, replace the coconut oil with coconut milk. Omit the salt.

Per serving: Calories: 279; Fat: 5g; Carbohydrates: 57g; Fiber: 3g; Protein: 33g; Sodium: 470mg; Iron: 9mg

RASPBERRY CHOCOLATE CHEESECAKE

SERVES 10 TO 12

Prep Time: 30 minutes, plus 30 minutes to 2 hours for chilling

● GLUTEN-FREE
● LEFTOVER-FRIENDLY
● PLAN AHEAD

FOR THE ALMOND OAT CRUST

1 cup packed pitted dates (12 large dates)

½ cup rolled oats

½ cup raw almonds

½ teaspoon sea salt

¾ cup vegan chocolate chips

FOR THE CHEESECAKE

2½ cups raw unsalted whole cashews, soaked, drained, and rinsed (see page 11)

¾ cup freshly squeezed lemon juice

¾ cup maple syrup

¼ cup water

2 tablespoons vanilla extract

¾ teaspoon sea salt

FOR THE RASPBERRY TOPPING

3 cups raspberries

2 tablespoons coconut sugar

Make it WFPB: Omit the salt from the crust and filling.

Substitution tip: For a firmer cheesecake, use ¼ cup refined coconut oil (for its neutral flavor) in place of the ¼ cup water for the filling.

Per serving: Calories: 363; Fat: 18g; Carbohydrates: 47g; Fiber: 5g; Protein: 8g; Sodium: 11mg; Iron: 3mg

This is one of those your-eyes-will-get-big kind of desserts. It's a true crowd-pleaser for vegans and omnivores alike! In fact, the comment I hear most about this cheesecake is, "it doesn't taste like the dairy kind—it's better." Although this recipe may seem involved, it's actually very easy to make and well worth the effort. Plus, it's healthy enough to double as breakfast. How cool is that?

1. Make the almond oat crust: In a food processor, combine the dates, oats, almonds, and salt. Process until the mixture begins to ball up and stick together. Spoon into a 10-inch baking pan or 8-inch round pie pan, pressing down firmly and evenly with the palms of your hands. This is the base layer. Sprinkle the chocolate chips (I use Lily's brand, stevia-sweetened chocolate chips) on top of the crust and place in the refrigerator to chill.

2. Meanwhile, make the cheesecake filling: In a blender, combine the cashews, lemon juice, maple syrup, water, vanilla, and salt. Blend until velvety smooth.

3. Remove the crust from the refrigerator and evenly spread the cheesecake filling on top of the crust and chocolate chips. Smooth out the top. Cover and chill in the refrigerator for several hours (or in the freezer for about 30 minutes) until firm.

4. To make the raspberry topping: In a bowl, combine the raspberries and coconut sugar. Stir very well, smashing the berries with your spoon until they're well broken up but not mushy.

5. When firm, cut the cheesecake into individual pieces and top with the macerated raspberries right before serving. Refrigerate leftovers in an airtight container for 4 to 5 days or freeze for up to 4 months.

SNEAKY CHOCOLATE CAKE

SERVES 9 TO 12

Prep Time: 20 minutes
Cook Time: 40 minutes

● LEFTOVER-FRIENDLY

FOR THE CAKE

Nonstick cooking spray (coconut or avocado oil)

1 cup unsweetened nondairy milk

1 cup coconut sugar

¼ cup peeled finely grated raw beet

¼ cup raw cacao powder

2 tablespoons sunflower oil

1 tablespoon vanilla extract

¼ teaspoon sea salt

1½ cups whole-wheat pastry flour

1 teaspoon baking soda

FOR THE FROSTING

2½ cups peeled and diced sweet potato

¾ cup creamy, unsalted almond butter

¾ cup maple syrup

½ cup raw cacao powder

2 tablespoons coconut sugar

2 tablespoons vanilla extract

¾ teaspoon sea salt

Why so sneaky? Because there are straight-up vegetables in this cake! You'll never know, though, I promise. It's so luscious that you'll think you're eating something far more decadent. I hadn't enjoyed cake for many years before creating this recipe, because I tend to avoid refined sugars and flours—so to me, this cake is life-changing. It's perfect for parties, special occasions, or just making a weeknight feel celebratory.

1. Preheat the oven to 350°F. Spray an 8-by-8-inch baking pan with oil and set aside.

2. Make the cake: In a large bowl, combine the milk, sugar, beet, cacao powder, oil, vanilla, and salt. Use an immersion blender to emulsify it (or blend in a blender and add back to the bowl). Add the flour and baking soda and whisk with a wire whisk, until thoroughly combined.

3. Pour into the baking pan and bake for 40 minutes, or until a toothpick inserted into the center comes out clean. Cool completely before frosting.

4. While the cake is baking, make the frosting: Fill a large pot with a few inches of water and bring to a boil. Place the sweet potatoes in a steaming basket inside the pot, cover, and steam over medium heat for 20 minutes, or until tender.

5. Transfer to a bowl and add the almond butter. Using an electric mixer, starting on low then increasing to high, whip until smooth. Add the maple syrup, cacao powder, sugar, vanilla, and salt, blending with the beaters as you go. Whip with the beaters for several minutes, until smooth and creamy.

6. Once the cake is cooled, frost evenly and cut into 9 to 12 squares. Refrigerate in an airtight container (or in the baking dish covered with plastic wrap) for 3 to 4 days.

Make It WFPB: Swap the oil in the cake ingredients for applesauce, and line the baking pan with parchment instead of greasing it. Omit the salt.

Variation tip: For a peanut butter twist, substitute peanut butter for the almond butter. You can also sprinkle crushed peanuts and chocolate chips over the top for even more peanut butter–chocolate flair.

Per serving: Calories: 153; Fat: 3g; Carbohydrates: 29g; Fiber: 3g; Protein: 3g; Sodium: 124mg; Iron: 1mg

Buckwheat Crisps, page 199

CHAPTER TWELVE
STAPLES

CHICKY SEASONING

MAKES 1½ CUPS

Prep Time: 5 minutes

○ 30 MINUTES OR LESS
◐ GLUTEN-FREE
● LEFTOVER-FRIENDLY
○ NUT-FREE

1 cup nutritional yeast

3 tablespoons onion granules or powder

3 tablespoons seasoned salt

2 tablespoons dried parsley flakes

2 teaspoons celery seed

2 teaspoons dried garlic granules or powder

1 teaspoon coconut sugar

1 teaspoon lemon pepper

1 teaspoon dried dill

1 teaspoon dried rosemary

½ teaspoon freshly ground black pepper

½ teaspoon ground white pepper

I stopped buying expensive, premade vegetarian chicken seasonings when I realized how easy it was to make my own. This seasoning works great as an all-purpose "chicken" flavoring and only takes five minutes to toss together. It's also healthy—totally free from suspicious ingredients and chock-full of B vitamins. If you're like me, you'll use this a lot, so feel free to whip up a double or triple batch. It's part of several recipes in this book and also great on popcorn, baked potatoes, or tofu. Turn it into a broth by stirring 1 tablespoon into a cup of water, and use it to make seasoned rice and soups and to sauté vegetables in place of oil.

In a medium bowl, mix the nutritional yeast, onion granules, salt, parsley, celery seed, garlic granules, sugar, lemon pepper, dill, rosemary, black pepper, and white pepper together until thoroughly combined. Alternatively, you can use my "cheater" method and place the ingredients in a glass mason jar, screw on the lid, and shake to combine. Store in an airtight container out of direct sunlight for several months.

———————————

Ingredient tip: If you're new to onion and garlic granules, here's the deal: They are granulated (think "tiny sand particles") and have a more pleasant flavor and texture than the powdered versions. They are often mislabeled as powder, too, so look for what visually presents itself as granules. However, if you can only find the powdered versions, they are fine to use as well.

Per serving (2 tablespoons): Calories: 27; Fat: 0g; Carbohydrates: 4g; Fiber: 1g; Protein: 3g; Sodium: 39mg; Iron: 1mg

BUCKWHEAT CRISPS

MAKES ABOUT 2 CUPS

Prep Time: 1 minute, plus overnight soaking time

Cook Time: 25 to 28 minutes

- ● GLUTEN-FREE
- ● LEFTOVER-FRIENDLY
- ○ NUT-FREE
- ○ WFPB

2 cups buckwheat

Buckwheat is such an underrated grain, so I love celebrating it with these nutrient-dense crisps. I keep them on hand to sprinkle over cereals, chia puddings, and even salads. They're great as "cereal" topped with Strawberry Mylk (page 28) or Chocolate Mylk (page 29), especially with some berries on top. They're also a key part of the Meal Prep Chia Breakfast Bowl (page 42). Have fun experimenting with these crunchy little nuggets.

1. In a medium bowl, cover the buckwheat in plenty of water and soak for about 8 hours. Drain and rinse until no bubbles remain.

2. Preheat the oven to 300°F.

3. Line two large baking sheets with parchment paper or silicone liners and spread the buckwheat out in a thin layer over both sheets.

4. Bake for 25 to 28 minutes, or until dry and crisp. Allow to cool, then store in an airtight container at room temperature for up to a month, or freeze for several months to prolong shelf life.

Variation tip: I like to make "raw" buckwheat crisps in my food dehydrator. To do this, follow step 1, then set your dehydrator to 105°F (that temperature maintains all of the enzymes in order to still consider this a "raw" dish). Lay out the buckwheat crisps over two lined dehydrator trays and dehydrate for 5 to 6 hours, or until dried and crisp. Follow the same storage instructions.

Per recipe: Calories: 567; Fat: 4g; Carbohydrates: 123g; Fiber: 17g; Protein: 19g; Sodium: 18mg; Iron: 5mg

PLANTSTRONG PARM

MAKES ABOUT 1½ CUPS

Prep Time: 5 minutes

○ 30 MINUTES OR LESS
◐ GLUTEN-FREE
● LEFTOVER-FRIENDLY

1½ cups raw walnut halves
¼ cup nutritional yeast
¾ teaspoon sea salt

Think of this as vegan fairy dust—something magical that you can sprinkle on (almost) anything to make it more delicious and nutrient-dense. It's easy to make up a big batch of this, and it stores indefinitely in the refrigerator. We like to sprinkle it on pasta, pizza, rice, and roasted or steamed vegetables, just to name a few. This topping is a great source of B vitamins and omega-3s. Enjoy in good health.

1. In a food processor, combine the walnuts, nutritional yeast, and salt and blend until the walnuts are very crumbly. Be careful not to over-blend, because you want fine crumbles, not paste. This won't take very long, so watch carefully and go slow.

2. Once you achieve the desired texture, refrigerate in an airtight container for up to 1 month.

Variation tip: For spicy Parmesan, add a dash of cayenne or red chili flakes to the mixture. You can also add some garlic granules (or peeled, fresh garlic) if you'd like a garlicky Parmesan.

Per serving (2 tablespoons): Calories: 88; Fat: 8g; Carbohydrates: 2g; Fiber: 1g; Protein: 3g; Sodium: 4mg; Iron: 1mg

AVOTILLO SAUCE

MAKES ABOUT 5 CUPS

Prep Time: 10 minutes
Cook Time: 5 minutes

- ○ 30 MINUTES OR LESS
- ◐ GLUTEN-FREE
- ● LEFTOVER-FRIENDLY
- ○ NUT-FREE

2 large poblano peppers, stemmed

1 small white or yellow onion, cut into thick slices

8 tomatillos (about 3½ cups)

2 large avocados, peeled and pitted

1 cup packed fresh cilantro

½ cup freshly squeezed lime juice

8 large garlic cloves, peeled

2 jalapeños, stems removed

2 teaspoons sea salt

This delicious, creamy avocado-tomatillo sauce is perfect on top of burritos, tacos, tostadas, or anything remotely Mexican. We love keeping a batch of this on hand at all times because it's a great (and healthy!) way to add pizzazz to simple meals.

1. In a large, dry skillet over medium-high heat, place the poblanos and onion slices. Allow to char by pressing down occasionally, resisting the urge to flip until charred underneath. Ensure that all sides of the peppers have been charred before removing from the pan. This should take a total of about 5 minutes.

2. In a blender, combine the charred onion and poblanos with the tomatillos, avocados, cilantro, lime juice, garlic, jalapeños, and salt and process until smooth. Refrigerate in an airtight container for about a week.

First-timer tip: You may be wondering if you can get away with bottled lime juice instead of fresh. While I won't show up at your house with a search team, I do ever-so-strongly suggest you spend the extra time to squeeze fresh limes. It tastes infinitely fresher and provides much greater nutrition. You can use a handheld juicer or electric juicer—or whip up a batch of lime juice in advance to store in the refrigerator (it'll keep for up to a week). If you're a citrus fiend like me, make a ton and freeze the excess in small batches for future citrus emergencies.

Per serving (2 tablespoons): Calories: 15; Fat: 1g; Carbohydrates: 1g; Fiber: 1g; Protein: 0g; Sodium: 1mg; Iron: 0mg

CLASSIC SALSA

MAKES ABOUT 5 CUPS

Prep Time: 10 minutes

○ 30 MINUTES OR LESS
◐ GLUTEN-FREE
● LEFTOVER-FRIENDLY
○ NUT-FREE

1 (28-ounce) can diced tomatoes

½ cup minced red onion

½ cup minced scallions, both white and green parts

¼ cup minced jalapeño

¼ cup chopped fresh cilantro

8 large garlic cloves, minced, pressed, or thinly sliced

1½ teaspoons sea salt

Ten minutes is all that it takes to whip up a batch of this flavorful, immune-boosting salsa—and it couldn't be more worth it. There's just nothing like fresh, homemade salsa for adding a vibrant kick to your food. We love to use this on tacos, tostadas, burritos, chimichangas, and even over beans and rice or baked potatoes. And of course, it's perfect for dipping chips into, especially if you've also got some Classic Guacamole (page 64) on hand.

1. Pour the tomatoes and their juices into a food processor or blender and blend briefly until fairly smooth, leaving in a bit of texture.

2. Transfer to an airtight container and stir in the onion, scallions, jalapeño, cilantro, garlic, and salt and refrigerate. If possible, allow the flavors to marry for several hours before serving. Refrigerate in an airtight container for 1 to 2 weeks.

Ingredient tip: You can adjust the heat level depending on how you cut up your jalapeño. If you prefer less heat, be sure to remove the seeds before adding to the salsa. If you're a heat-lover, leave those seeds in—and maybe even add a little more jalapeño, or another hot pepper such as habanero or cayenne.

Variation tip: Add a squeeze of lime just before serving for a zingy citrus bite.

Per serving (1 cup): Calories: 60; Fat: 0g; Carbohydrates: 13g; Fiber: 4g; Protein: 2g; Sodium: 371mg; Iron: 0mg

CASHEW-MACADAMIA CHEESE

MAKES ABOUT 3 CUPS

Prep Time: 5 to 10 minutes

- GLUTEN-FREE
- LEFTOVER-FRIENDLY
- PLAN AHEAD

1 cup macadamia nuts

1 cup raw unsalted whole cashews, soaked, drained, and rinsed (see page 11)

¾ cup water

¼ cup nutritional yeast

¼ cup freshly squeezed lemon juice

3 large garlic cloves, peeled

1 teaspoon sea salt

⅛ teaspoon ground white pepper

This nondairy cheese is delicious as a dip for crackers or raw veggies, or as an alternative to processed cheeses in wraps, sandwiches, lasagna, and pizza. For a special treat, top a baked tortilla (or sprouted raw tortilla) with a layer of this cheese and sprinkle with Walnut-Quinoa Crumbles (page 124), sun-dried tomatoes, spinach, fresh basil, and olives.

In a blender or food processor, combine the macadamia nuts, cashews, water, nutritional yeast, lemon juice, garlic, salt, and white pepper. Blend until velvety smooth. Refrigerate in an airtight container for at least 2 weeks.

Ingredient tip: If you have a high-speed blender (such as a Vitamix or Blendtec), you don't need to soak the cashews beforehand. Typically, macadamias don't need to be soaked because they're such a soft nut, but you can also soak them along with the cashews if your blender isn't making this dip perfectly smooth.

Per serving (2 tablespoons): Calories: 28; Fat: 2g; Carbohydrates: 1g; Fiber: 0g; Protein: 0g; Sodium: 1mg; Iron: 0mg

CASHEW RANCH DRESSING

MAKES ABOUT 1½ CUPS

Prep Time: 5 minutes

- GLUTEN-FREE
- LEFTOVER-FRIENDLY
- PLAN AHEAD

1½ cups raw unsalted whole cashews, soaked, drained, and rinsed (see page 11)

1 cup water

2½ tablespoons apple cider vinegar

2 large garlic cloves, peeled

4 teaspoons onion granules or powder

¾ teaspoon sea salt

1 tablespoon dried parsley

1½ teaspoons dried dill

Ranch dressing that's actually vegan—and healthy? Did you just die and go to heaven? Probably not, but this creamy and delicious dressing will make you think so and will be a fantastic addition to your plant-based kitchen. We love to use this dressing as a dip for raw veggies, Buffalo cauliflower, and in sandwiches and wraps. Of course, it's also the perfect way to make a salad more enticing, such as in the Vegan Cobb Salad (page 91). This dressing was a huge hit with my recipe testers, because even those with picky kids said that absolutely *everyone* loved it. What a great way to entice people to eat more vegetables.

1. In a blender, combine the cashews, water, vinegar, garlic, onion granules, and salt, and process until smooth and velvety.

2. Transfer to a container and stir in the parsley and dill. Cover with a tight-fitting lid and refrigerate for up to 2 weeks. This dressing will thicken a bit once chilled overnight. If necessary, add a little water to thin.

Variation tip: If you'd like to make the Cashew Ranch Dressing a pretty shade of green, add a small handful of spinach leaves to the blender.

Per serving (2 tablespoons): Calories: 93; Fat: 7g; Carbohydrates: 6g; Fiber: 1g; Protein: 3g; Sodium: 4mg; Iron: 1mg

CHIPOTLE CREAM SAUCE

MAKES ABOUT 1½ CUPS

Prep Time: 10 minutes

- ◐ GLUTEN-FREE
- ● LEFTOVER-FRIENDLY
- ○ PLAN AHEAD

1 cup raw unsalted whole cashews, soaked, drained, and rinsed (see page 11)

½ cup water

¼ cup freshly squeezed lime juice

2 tablespoons coconut sugar

2 tablespoons nutritional yeast

1 teaspoon dried chipotle powder

½ teaspoon sea salt

This smooth, mellow, slightly spicy sauce is absolutely essential in our kitchen. We use it regularly to make Avocado Toast with Chipotle Cream Sauce (page 48) and to jazz up burritos, tacos, and tostadas. It can even stand in as a salad dressing, when thinned down a bit with extra water. It basically makes any Mexican dish you can imagine even better—think of this as the little sauce that could.

1. In a blender, place the drained cashews along with the water, lime juice, coconut sugar, nutritional yeast, chipotle, and salt. Blend until completely smooth and emulsified.

2. Refrigerate in an airtight container for up to 2 weeks.

Ingredient tip: You can find chipotle powder in any health food store and in most supermarkets. I used Frontier brand in this recipe. It's also great for sprinkling on stir-fried vegetables for fajitas, tacos, or burritos.

Make it WFPB: Omit the salt.

Per serving (2 tablespoons): Calories: 73; Fat: 5g; Carbohydrates: 6g; Fiber: 1g; Protein: 3g; Sodium: 3mg; Iron: 1mg

PEANUT SAUCE, TWO WAYS

MAKES ABOUT 1 CUP

Prep Time: 10 minutes

○ 30 MINUTES OR LESS
◐ GLUTEN-FREE
● LEFTOVER-FRIENDLY

FOR THE LOWER-FAT PEANUT BUTTER POWDER VERSION

½ cup peanut butter powder

2 tablespoons tamari, shoyu, or soy sauce

2 tablespoons freshly squeezed lime juice

2 large garlic cloves, minced or pressed

1 tablespoon finely grated or minced fresh ginger

2 tablespoons maple syrup

1 teaspoon toasted sesame oil

2 tablespoons water

1 teaspoon sriracha sauce (optional)

FOR THE PEANUT BUTTER VERSION

½ cup peanut butter

¼ cup plus 2 tablespoons coconut sugar

¼ cup plus 2 tablespoons water

3 tablespoons tamari, shoyu, or soy sauce

2 tablespoons finely grated or minced fresh ginger

1 tablespoon apple cider vinegar

1 tablespoon toasted sesame oil

3 large garlic cloves, minced or pressed

Sea salt

Here I present to you not one, but two absolutely luscious peanut sauces. Both versions are delicious, but I wanted to give you options because it's nice to have a lower-fat version of peanut sauce if you have access to high-quality peanut butter powder. I like to keep at least one of these on hand at all times, because I love Fresh Spring Rolls with Peanut Sauce (page 77). It's also a quick way to dress up brown rice, noodles, and salads. I strongly suggest making a double or triple batch of peanut sauce, especially if you're cooking for a crowd.

In a bowl, combine all of the ingredients and whisk well to combine. If you're using salted peanut butter, you probably won't need the additional salt. If you prefer a completely smooth result, you can blend the ingredients in a blender instead. Refrigerate sauces in an airtight container for 1 to 2 weeks.

Make it WFPB: Omit the sesame oil in either recipe and add an equal portion of water. Use an unsalted peanut butter if making the peanut butter version and skip the additional salt.

Ingredient tip: You can find peanut butter powder in just about any supermarket, but I love buying it from health food stores in bulk (I get mine at Natural Grocers), because it's free from sugar and unnecessary ingredients, cheaper, *and* organic. Great combo!

Per serving (2 tablespoons of the Lower-Fat Peanut Butter Powder Version): Calories: 46; Fat: 1g; Carbohydrates: 7g; Fiber: 1g; Protein: 3g; Sodium: 36mg; Iron: 0mg

LOW-FAT CHEESE DIP

SERVES 4

Prep Time: 10 minutes

● GLUTEN-FREE
● LEFTOVER-FRIENDLY
● PLAN AHEAD

1 (15-ounce) can white beans, rinsed and drained, or 1½ cups cooked white beans (see page 17)

¼ cup nutritional yeast

¼ cup raw, unsalted cashew pieces, soaked and drained (see page 11)

¼ cup jarred roasted red peppers

2 tablespoons freshly squeezed lemon juice

2 tablespoons water

2 large garlic cloves, peeled

½ teaspoon sea salt

This tangy cheese dip is low in fat, but definitely not low in flavor. I consider it one of my "transformation" recipes, and here's why—I recently had a client who needed help overhauling her cooking and eating habits. She wanted to lose weight, but absolutely hated beans. *Every kind of bean.* By some miracle, I got her to try this recipe, which is chock-full of beans, and (drumroll, please), she absolutely loved it—and even proceeded to go home and make herself a double batch! I'll never forget that high-five moment after she realized she could, in fact, enjoy health-promoting beans if they were made to taste like this. Use this delicious cheese in sandwiches, tacos, or wraps, or simply as a dip for crackers, tortilla chips, or raw veggies.

In a blender, combine the white beans, nutritional yeast, cashews, roasted red peppers, lemon juice, water, garlic, and salt. Blend until smooth and velvety. Serve cold or at room temperature. Refrigerate in an airtight container for about a week.

Ingredient tip: Sometimes I buy cashew pieces, sometimes whole cashews. Either are fine, but here's the reason I specify in my recipes: Whole cashews take up more space in a measuring cup, while the pieces settle into the cups more, so there is a slight difference when measuring them. I recommend keeping both on hand.

Per serving: Calories: 160; Fat: 4g; Carbohydrates: 23g; Fiber: 6g; Protein: 10g; Sodium: 252mg; Iron: 2mg

CHEESY SAUCE

MAKES 3 CUPS DRY MIX, AND 9 CUPS SAUCE

Prep Time: 5 to 10 minutes

Cook Time: 2 minutes

○ 30 MINUTES OR LESS
◐ GLUTEN-FREE
● LEFTOVER-FRIENDLY

FOR THE DRY CHEESY MIX

1¼ cups nutritional yeast

1 cup raw unsalted cashew pieces

½ cup rolled oats

¼ cup arrowroot powder

2 tablespoons seasoned salt

2 tablespoons garlic granules or powder

1½ tablespoons onion granules or powder

½ teaspoon ground turmeric

FOR THE CHEESY SAUCE

1 cup Dry Cheesy Mix

2 cups water, divided

¼ cup grated carrots

¼ cup jarred roasted red peppers

This sauce is life. In fact, we're so dependent on it that we always keep the dry mix on hand and often have the liquid version ready to go, too. We love this on steamed veggies, tacos, tostadas, burritos, brown rice, nachos, baked (or air-fried) french fries, and more. For an easy meal, you can even top a baked potato with broccoli and smother it in this nutritious, scrumptious sauce. Yum-o-rama!

TO MAKE THE DRY CHEESY MIX

In a food processor, place the nutritional yeast, cashews, oats, arrowroot, salt, garlic granules, onion granules, and turmeric. Blend into a fine powder. At this point, you can store the dry mix in the refrigerator in an airtight container for a month or more. It can also be frozen for many months.

TO MAKE THE CHEESY SAUCE

1. In a blender, combine the Dry Cheesy Mix, 1 cup water, carrots, and red peppers and blend on low until as smooth as possible. Add the remaining cup water and blend well. Increase to high speed and blend until very smooth.

2. Transfer to a medium pot. Heat the sauce over medium heat. Cook for about 2 minutes, whisking often, until thickened. Serve warm.

Batch cooking tip: I formulated this recipe to make a large quantity of the dry mix to keep on hand in the refrigerator or freezer. Once you have it made, it takes less than 5 minutes to transform it into velvety, warm cheese sauce. When I know I'll be using lots of Cheesy Sauce for the week, I'll blend up the whole sauce and keep it refrigerated. It lasts this way for up to 1 week, and only takes a minute to whisk into a thick sauce on the stove—perfect for busy nights!

Per serving (1 cup Cheesy Sauce): Calories: 48; Fat: 2g; Carbohydrates: 6g; Fiber: 1g; Protein: 2g; Sodium: 331mg; Iron: 1mg

EAT-IT-EVERY-DAY GRAVY

MAKES ABOUT 6 CUPS

Prep Time: 10 minutes
Cook Time: 45 minutes

● GLUTEN-FREE
● LEFTOVER-FRIENDLY
● PLAN AHEAD

8 ounces portobello mushrooms
(4 cups), chopped

1 large white onion, chopped (2½ cups)

1 cup walnuts

1 (15-ounce) can navy beans, rinsed and
drained, or 1½ cups cooked navy beans
(see page 17)

¼ cup tamari, shoyu, or soy sauce

¼ cup nutritional yeast

¼ cup Chicky Seasoning (page 198)

3 tablespoons balsamic vinegar

5 large garlic cloves, peeled

1 tablespoon dried rosemary

1 teaspoon dried sage

½ teaspoon freshly ground black pepper

2 cups water, divided

Variation tip: One of my favorite alternative
takes on this recipe is to use shiitake
mushrooms instead of the portobellos. Or,
do half and half.

Per serving (2 tablespoons): Calories:
8; Fat: 0g; Carbohydrates: 1g; Fiber: 0g;
Protein: 1g; Sodium: 16mg; Iron: 0mg

Gravy isn't just for special occasions anymore. This whole-foods, plant-strong recipe is easy to make, especially if you keep the Chicky Seasoning (page 198) on hand. It's great served over mashed potatoes (duh), but also over Everything Tofu (page 212), brown rice, quinoa, baked or roasted potatoes, and even noodles. I like to keep a big batch on hand because it makes weeknight meals so much easier, and tastier, too. The consistency of this gravy is a bit thicker than other gravies I've had that were loaded with excess oils, but the taste is phenomenal, and you can feel great about eating this, yes, every single day.

1. Preheat the oven to 400°F.

2. On a large nonstick baking sheet or baking sheet lined with a silicone liner or parchment paper, place the mushrooms and onion in a single layer.

3. Bake for 25 minutes. Remove from the oven, stir, and bake for an additional 20 minutes, or until the mushrooms and onion are very tender and beginning to brown.

4. In a blender, combine the walnuts, beans, tamari, nutritional yeast, Chicky Seasoning, vinegar, garlic, rosemary, sage, and pepper. Add the mushrooms and onions and ½ cup of the water. Blend until as smooth as possible.

5. Slowly add the remaining 1½ cups water, and blend until velvety smooth. To serve, warm briefly in a pan. Refrigerate in an airtight container for up to a week or freeze for a few months.

EVERYTHING TOFU

SERVES 4 TO 6

Prep Time: 2 to 3 minutes
Cook Time: 40 to 45 minutes

◐ GLUTEN-FREE
● LEFTOVER-FRIENDLY
○ NUT-FREE

1 pound extra-firm tofu

2 tablespoons tamari, shoyu, or soy sauce

2 teaspoons garlic granules or powder

2 teaspoons toasted sesame oil

This easy-peasy tofu goes great with—wait for it—everything! Put it on top of salads, noodles, rice dishes, quinoa, and stir-fries. It's also great inside the Fresh Spring Rolls with Peanut Sauce (see page 77), or as the filling for a simple vegetable wrap—place shredded veggies, this tofu, and some Low-Fat Cheese Dip (page 208) or Cashew Ranch Dressing (page 205) in a whole-grain tortilla, and you're in business. If you have an air fryer, these will cook up beautifully there, too—in about half the time.

1. Preheat the oven to 400°F. Line a large baking sheet with parchment paper or a silicone liner and set aside.

2. Pour off the excess water from the tofu package and slice it horizontally into 6 rectangular slabs. Press the tofu (see page 14), then cut into cubes between ½- and 1-inch thick.

3. Place the tofu cubes in a medium bowl and sprinkle evenly with the tamari, garlic granules, and oil. Toss gently with a rubber spatula to evenly coat the tofu.

4. Spread the tofu cubes on the prepared baking sheet, leaving room in between each so that they're not touching each other. Bake for 40 to 45 minutes, or until golden brown. Remove and serve warm or hot. Refrigerate in an airtight container for several days.

Make it WFPB: Omit the sesame oil and proceed with the recipe without any substitutions.

Per serving: Calories: 134; Fat: 8g; Carbohydrates: 4g; Fiber: 1g; Protein: 14g; Sodium: 347mg; Iron: 2mg

CAULIFLOWER TACO MEAT

SERVES 4

Prep Time: 5 minutes
Cook Time: 10 minutes

- ○ 30 MINUTES OR LESS
- ◐ GLUTEN-FREE
- ● LEFTOVER-FRIENDLY
- ○ NUT-FREE

1 tablespoon sunflower or olive oil

2 cups riced cauliflower

3 large garlic cloves, minced or pressed

2 tablespoons nutritional yeast

1 tablespoon tamari, shoyu, or soy sauce

2 teaspoons onion granules or powder

1½ teaspoons salt-free chili powder

1 teaspoon ground cumin

½ teaspoon dried oregano

Cauliflower "meat?" Has the world gone cauliflower-crazy? Yes, and rightly so. It's a great way to "cheat" in more vegetables and still feel like you're eating something very satisfying. I love to use these crumbles in tacos, burritos, salads, tostadas, and anywhere else taco meat might appear. They're especially yummy when paired with creamy refried beans, as they add another texture and flavor. You may wish to double or triple this recipe, as it freezes well and is so nice to have on hand.

1. In a large pan, heat the oil over medium-high heat. When it's just begun to shimmer, add the riced cauliflower, garlic, nutritional yeast, tamari, onion granules, chili powder, cumin, and oregano. Cook for about 10 minutes, stirring often, until the cauliflower is very tender and all of the moisture has been absorbed.

2. Serve warm or hot. Refrigerate leftovers in an airtight container for up to a week or freeze for up to 4 months.

Make it WFPB: Omit the oil and use water or vegetable broth.

Ingredient tip: This recipe works just as well with a 12-ounce bag of frozen cauliflower rice. I love the convenience of that option (we buy the large organic bags at Costco), but if you'd like to make your own, just whirl raw cauliflower in your food processor until crumbly and rice-sized (or take a cheese grater to it).

Per serving: Calories: 61; Fat: 4g; Carbohydrates: 5g; Fiber: 2g; Protein: 3g; Sodium: 214mg; Iron: 1mg

MEASUREMENT CONVERSIONS

VOLUME EQUIVALENTS (LIQUID)

STANDARD	US STANDARD (OUNCES)	METRIC (APPROXIMATE)
2 tablespoons	1 fl. oz.	30 mL
¼ cup	2 fl. oz.	60 mL
½ cup	4 fl. oz.	120 mL
1 cup	8 fl. oz.	240 mL
1½ cups	12 fl. oz.	355 mL
2 cups or 1 pint	16 fl. oz.	475 mL
4 cups or 1 quart	32 fl. oz.	1 L
1 gallon	128 fl. oz.	4 L

OVEN TEMPERATURES

FAHRENHEIT (F)	CELSIUS (C) (APPROXIMATE)
250°	120°
300°	150°
325°	165°
350°	180°
375°	190°
400°	200°
425°	220°
450°	230°

VOLUME EQUIVALENTS (DRY)

STANDARD	METRIC (APPROXIMATE)
⅛ teaspoon	0.5 mL
¼ teaspoon	1 mL
½ teaspoon	2 mL
¾ teaspoon	4 mL
1 teaspoon	5 mL
1 tablespoon	15 mL
¼ cup	59 mL
⅓ cup	79 mL
½ cup	118 mL
⅔ cup	156 mL
¾ cup	177 mL
1 cup	235 mL
2 cups or 1 pint	475 mL
3 cups	700 mL
4 cups or 1 quart	1 L

WEIGHT EQUIVALENTS

STANDARD	METRIC (APPROXIMATE)
½ ounce	15 g
1 ounce	30 g
2 ounces	60 g
4 ounces	115 g
8 ounces	225 g
12 ounces	340 g
16 ounces or 1 pound	455 g

RESOURCES

FILMS

Cowspiracy: The Sustainability Secret, Kip Andersen and Keegan Kuhn, 2014

> A surprising look at why more environmental organizations don't promote a vegan diet.

Forks Over Knives, Lee Fulkerson, 2011

> A compelling documentary about the connection between animal products and health problems.

The Game Changers, Louie Psihoyos, 2018

> An entertaining and powerful documentary about vegan athletes and the benefits of a plant-based diet.

What the Health, Kip Andersen and Keegan Kuhn, 2017

> By the same people who brought us *Cowspiracy*, this documentary uncovers the truth behind many of the largest "health" organizations.

BOOKS

Barnard, Dr. Neal. *Dr. Neal Barnard's Program for Reversing Diabetes*. Rodale Books, 2006.

Campbell, T. Colin. *The China Study*. Dallas: BenBella Books, 2004.

Challis, Tess. *The Essential Vegan Air Fryer Cookbook*. Emeryville, CA: Rockridge Press, 2019.

Challis, Tess. *FOOD LOVE*. CreateSpace Independent Publishing, 2016.

Challis, Tess. *Radiance 4 Life*. Pagosa Springs, CO: Quintessential Health Publishing, 2011.

Challis, Tess. *Radiant Health, Inner Wealth*. Pagosa Springs, CO: Quintessential Health Publishing, 2009.

Challis, Tess. *The Two-Week Wellness Solution*. Pagosa Springs, CO: Quintessential Health Publishing, 2010.

Challis, Tess. *Vegan Mediterranean Cookbook*. Emeryville, CA: Rockridge Press, 2019.

Cornbleet, Jennifer. *Raw Food Made Easy for 1 or 2 People*. Book Publishing Company, 2005.

Wood, Rebecca. *The New Whole Foods Encyclopedia: A Comprehensive Resource for Healthy Eating*. New York: Penguin Books, 2010.

APPS

Yelp and Happy Cow are two apps I use when traveling to find good local vegan eateries.

COACHING

Vanessa at plantbasedmuscles.com is someone I've personally trained with. I'd highly recommend her for increasing your motivation and personal fitness.

Will Tucker is another excellent vegan fitness trainer. You can find him at willtuckerfitness .trainerize.com.

My website is TessChallis.com. I do life, health, and business coaching using my "one degree" method.

REFERENCES

Dr. McDougall's Health and Medical Center. "Osteoporosis." Accessed on December 15, 2019. https://www.drmcdougall .com/health/education/health-science /common-health-problems/osteoporosis/

Healthline. "11 Reasons Why Too Much Sugar is Bad for You." Accessed on December 15, 2019. https://www.healthline.com /nutrition/too-much-sugar#section6

Martin, David S. 2011. "The 'Heart Attack Proof' Diet?" CNN, Accessed on December 15, 2019. http://www.cnn .com/2011/HEALTH/08/19/heart.attack .proof.diet/index.html

Medical News Today. "Going Vegan Could Prevent Type 2 Diabetes." Accessed on December 15, 2019. https://www .medicalnewstoday.com/articles /320909.php#4

Medical News Today. "Top 15 Sources of Plant-Based Protein." Accessed on January 17, 2020. https://www.medical newstoday.com/articles/321474.php

Physician's Committee for Responsible Medicine. "Calcium and Strong Bones." Accessed on January 17, 2020. https://www.pcrm.org /good-nutrition/nutrition-information /health-concerns-about-dairy/calcium -and-strong-bones

Physician's Committee for Responsible Medicine. "Vegan Diets Reduce the Risk of Chronic Disease." Accessed on December 15, 2019. https://www.pcrm.org/news /health-nutrition/vegan-diets-reduce-risk -chronic-disease

INDEX

ACKNOWLEDGMENTS

This is actually my favorite part of writing a book, because I get to thank all the awesome humans who supported this process!

As always, big props to my fabulous recipe testers. You ladies helped make this book so much better with all of your feedback. Thank you so stinkin' much! Mandi Barstow, Coreen Saito, Kristen Cowgill, Leslie Finnegan Conn, Kassidy Bennett, Kristina Martin, Jan Cawthorne, Michelle Wilson, Erin Petschke, Jan Nicolet, Alesha Kay Flynn, Angela Marie, Nicole Lueders, and Adrian Jordan-Ford, your input was invaluable.

In my own kitchen, I get to cook with (and for) my wonderful partner John and my darling daughter, Alethea, who both have exceptionally refined palates that I trust. Your support, feedback, encouragement, and excitement about these recipes means so much to me. I was also lucky to test a few recipes alongside my cousin and soul sister Stacia Aashna, who helped make the book even better. I love and appreciate you three brilliant beings more than you know.

I'm also grateful to the well-oiled machine that is my publishing house, Callisto. You guys are amazing, and I appreciate every one of you.

And finally, I want to acknowledge you, the reader. Thank you for holding my newest book baby in your hands—I hope you love it as much as I do. I appreciate you so much!

ABOUT THE AUTHOR

 A "One Degree Transformation Specialist," eight-time author, life and business coach, and speaker, **Tess Challis** helps people create their own recipe for success, in food and in life—one doable step at a time. She's been featured in *Huffington Post*, *Mind Body Green*, and on television networks including ABC, NBC, and CBS. Tess lives in Phoenix, Arizona, and combats the heat by drinking a bit too much kombucha. Get inspiration, recipes, and more at TessChallis.com.

CPSIA information can be obtained
at www.ICGtesting.com
Printed in the USA
BVHW020844280420
578706BV00010B/111